ISBN: 9781313919623

Published by:
HardPress Publishing
8345 NW 66TH ST #2561
MIAMI FL 33166-2626

Email: info@hardpress.net
Web: http://www.hardpress.net

CANADA'S WEST
AND
FARTHER WEST

CANADA'S WEST
AND
FARTHER WEST
By FRANK CARREL, Journalist

LATEST BOOK ON THE
LAND OF GOLDEN
OPPORTUNITIES

PUBLISHED AND PRINTED BY
THE TELEGRAPH PRINTING COMPANY
QUEBEC, 1911

W
MAH

TO

SIR WM. MAX AITKEN, M.P.

MANY impressions of Western Canada have been published by authors of note, but in the following pages the writer, in a humble way, has endeavored to recount how much can be seen, how much ground can be covered and how much information can be gathered, in a month's journey from Quebec to Victoria, via the inland lakes, and over the Canadian Pacific, Grand Trunk and Canadian Northern Railways, with side trips down the Okanagan Valley, Yoho Valley and Crow's Nest. To all the foregoing transportation companies and many old and new Western friends, the writer is indebted for many of the accompanying photographs and statistics, which are at all times gladly and willingly given to all visitors from the East, for there are no more hospitable people in the world to-day than the Canadian Westerners.

THE AUTHOR.

Missing Page

TABLE OF CONTENTS

PAGE

TABLE OF ILLUSTRATIONS

TABLE OF ILLUSTRATIONS

TABLE OF ILLUSTRATIONS

TABLE OF ILLUSTRATIONS

TABLE OF ILLUSTRATIONS

CANADA'S WEST
AND
FARTHER WEST

CHAPTER I

Quebec to Port Arthur—Fort William

In August of the year 1909, we left Quebec for an extended trip through the West of Canada, which is now so widely known throughout the world, that it would be superfluous to mention in detail the various villages, towns, and cities, and the thousands of miles of railway and boat travel, which such a journey must necessarily impose upon the traveller.

Our trip had no other object except that of sight-seeing and the gathering of information and impressions for the readers of the Telegraph. We had heard and read so much of this Great West, which, by the way, is a very large part of this vast Northern Continent known as the Dominion of Canada. Time

1

and again the " Call of the West " had appeal-
ed to us, first with the alluring discoveries of
gold and silver, and secondly by the exciting
stories of the march of civilization, the development of the wheat centres, the birth and
rapid growth of villages, towns and cities.
We resisted the spirit of the first impulse, but
we willingly fell victims to the second, and
from Quebec we wended our way by boat to
Montreal, and from there by Grand Trunk
Railway to Sarnia, and so on to the Pacific
Coast.

-That we had so long deferred our visit to
the West was a constant source of surprise to,
and of comment by people whom we met in
our wanderings in Europe.

" You don't mean to say that you have
never seen the Rocky Mountains ? " we have
been asked, hundreds of times, and on how
many occasions have we heard casual travelling acquaintances remark: " Strange, indeed,
that you are travelling so far away from home
when you have not seen the grandest part of
your own country. "

At last we were so enthused over this great
land of promise, that we determined to see it
before its further development, in order that
we could revisit it again and see the still
greater advance and progress that will be visible in another ten or twelve years.

We left home keyed to a high note of expect-
ancy of seeing wonderful things, but somehow

2

or other we felt that the realization would be greater than our preconceptions. We had no programme, and we purchased railway transportation only from point to point.

Edmonton was our first destination, and we took the most pleasant way of reaching it, that is, we used the railway route as much as was convenient, but we must not omit to mention the delightful experience of our steamer travel from Sarnia to Port Arthur on the "Harmonia" the latest addition to the Northern Navigation Company's fleet of palatial lake steamers.

We left Toronto at 8 a.m. and arrived at Sarnia about two o'clock the same afternoon. We carried our baggage, or that portion the porter could not carry, from the special train which had brought us from Toronto, on board the majestic lake boat, lying at the dock, when we suddenly remembered that we had not as yet made any reservations for cabin accommodation. There were quite a number of passengers similarly deficient, so we got into line, a very long one, reaching several times round the vast rotunda of the ship, and for an hour patiently waited our turn, during which time the ship slipped its moorings. The women, as usual, won the honors for taking up the time of the purser.

The purser was helpless to oblige us with an ordinary cabin, or even a berth. Suspecting that there might he some special cabins still " unreserved ", we offered to take one at any price, provided we could be alone. The purser smiled, and asked if we would take the " official " suite. We said we never went back on our word for in this instance we felt we would be the gainer in every respect. To which he replied, " Well, I don't know about that, as it will cost you $17.00 extra for the two days' sail. "

It was worth every dollar of that sum, and a good deal more when we realized the crowded state of the boat, and the luxury which surrounded us in our cabin. It was one of a dozen or more on the top deck, with decorations and other comforts equal to the most elaborate hotel suites that are provided for Dukes, Barons and Counts because of their titles, and for the other fellows who have the wealth. It was one of those sort of rooms panelled with embossed ornamentations in pretty squares and circles. The ceiling was divided with raised floral wreathing, and studded with small electric lights. The covering of the brass bedsteads, was of rich design, and seductive enough to meet the fancy of any human being. The only thing that might have kept us awake at night was the price of the room, but then it did not, so quickly acquired are extravagant habits.

We had a large number of passengers on board, mostly Canadians, with a scattering of Americans, the former destined for Port

4

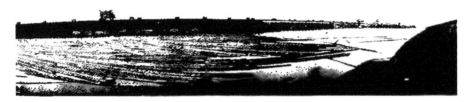

1. Canadian Northern Ry. Terminals. Port Arthur. Ont.
2. Canadian Northern Ry. Coal Dock—View from the Ironworks.
Port Arthur, Ont.
3. Coal Docks, Port Arthur, Ont.

Arthur and Fort William, and the latter for Duluth, Minn. It was a quiet and most orderly crowd, and everything was arranged for our comfort on board. There was a piano and a good hardwood floor in the observation parlor, but no dancing or singing. Everyone was satisfied to sit and enjoy the peacefulness of the afternoon and evening on Lake Huron, the fascination of the latter being enhanced with the rising moon. At 10.30 p. m. all was quiet and only the splashing of the waters of the lake, against our inpenetrable steel fortress could be heard.

Sault Ste. Marie was reached at noon the next day, where more passengers embarked, and a small quantity of freight was taken on. Then we proceeded in a North Westerly direction until we reached Lake Superior, the largest of all the inland lakes.

We passed hundreds of freight boats loaded down with ore from the iron ranges north of Duluth, some of these boats measuring over six hundred feet. We also passed several passenger steamers going in the opposite direction, among them, Jim Hill's "Northland," which up to the time of the launching of the "Harmonia", was considered the finest boat on the lakes.

We reached Port Arthur about 9.30 next morning, on a truly beautiful day, the picture in front of us resembling somewhat the entrance to some European port, with the two cities, Fort William and Port Arthur, guarded from the turbulent seas by a fine breakwater.

We were not favorably impressed with Port Arthur, but were told that it was destined to be a great city in the future, particularly when the Canadian Northern have completed their programme for its further development.

The citizens were excited with the prospect of a million dollar hotel to be erected shortly by the Canadian Northern Railway, which had been presented with a piece of property worth as much more in the centre of the city. Port Arthur had just completed a pretty theatre and a Carnegie Library, while preparations were being made for the laying of a corner stone of a Masonic Temple which was to surpass all other structures in the city. There was a building being erected to cost $25,000, and another coal dock, but the big features of Port Arthur's and Fort William's future are the growth of their grain elevators. Both towns lie close to one another and already boast of several grain elevators to take care of the grain exports of Western Canada.

When the histories of these two cities are placed in the archives of the country, they will make interesting reading, for no two cities in the West have spent so much (for their size) in a competitive war to outdo one another.

For Easterners to readily understand the

6

importance of both these towns, it must be mentioned that all the grain grown in the West, and that amounts to over one hundred and twenty-five millions of bushels this year alone, (not including oats, barley, etc.,) has to be shipped to the East, where a large quantity (about two-thirds), is forwarded for export to foreign markets. Now these two ports offer the greatest convenience to the railways for covering a large portion of the carriage by lake transportation, and thereby saving the extra freight charges of a railway haul. This fact was first demonstrated by the Canadian Pacific Railway, which began the shipment of grain in 1884 ; then the Canadian Northern Railway followed, and now the Grand Trunk Pacific is completing its terminals to join in line with the other two transcontinantal roads.

From a report of the Historical Society of Fort William, concerning the first shipment of grain, we extract from a report of Mr. John King, at present a citizen of Fort William and a retired merchant ,the following :

" In the fall and winter of 1883–84 we unloaded the first grain crop that came from the West with wheelbarrows into a shed built on the Kaministiquia River at the Westfort. In the Spring grain was loaded again with wheelbarrows. The first year we unloaded about half a million bushels. The same year the Canadian Pacific Railway built a track from Westfort to Eastfort, now called Fort William. There was a small station built also. "

A short time ago the Canadian Northern's elevator at Port Arthur, with a capacity of over a million bushels, had the distinction of being the largest in the world. Now the Grand Trunk Pacific is building a unit of one which will accommodate ten millions of bushels.

1. Steamer Lake Superior, of Northern Navigation Co'y.
2. Fort William—10,000,000 bushels elevator under construction.
3. Main Street, Fort William.

CHAPTER II

Port Arthur—Fort William

THE SITUATIONS of Port Arthur and Fort William are exceptionally adapted for making them important lake ports. The land in this vicinity is flat and the soil soft, which permits of the dredging of canals and the building of docks and ship yards at a minimum cost.

"Nature and the Government have done everything for Fort William" remarked a gentleman, "and what they have not done is now being accomplished for the Grand Trunk Pacific Company by the Lake Superior Terminal Co."

"This is a stupendous work, and with the building of the new elevator, the reclaiming of two hundred and fifty-three acres of land, the dredging of canals, laying out of car yards, there will be spent in the neighborhood of three millions of dollars."

We asked our informant, one of the energetic resident engineers of the Lake Superior Terminals, of the Grand Trunk Pacific, when he expected all this work to be completed?

"Never," he replied, "it will go on forever. When that part which we are building to-day is complete, the increase of trade will warrant a continuation of more yards, docks, and elevators, and when Fort William and Port Arthur become allied to one another in making themselves a great and growing industrial centre of Western Ontario, this work of dock improvements will have to be continued. "

As far as we could judge, our informant was not far wrong in his calculations of the future. We could observe from where we stood the huge elevator to accommodate three millions eight hundred thousand bushels of grain, in course of erection, and the general transformation of what was a huge marsh into the most modern looking railway yard, and thus we realized what it would develop into in the very near future. None however but those engaged in the transportations problems of the West have any conception of the enormously increasing crops, and the difficulties which will have to be surmounted to keep pace with the demands which will be made upon the three large railway corporations who are now vieing with one another in making preparations to handle the business. Those who are acquainted with the statistics of the annually increasing traffic of the railways of the West, say, that the railway traffic of that part of Canada will he more than doubled within five years, and when the immense works in course of erection, or preparation at Fort William to meet the demands, are completed, it is more than probable that the traffic will have so increased as to test them to their full capacity, or accommodation. It would seem to us that all these problems have been taken into consideration by the Grand Trunk Pacific in their present preparations at this point. The engineers know it, and are enthusiastic over their work. We conversed with the superintendent and foremen of the elevators, and other works, and found them ever ready to respond to our queries, and as enthusiastically as though they were personally interested in the construction going on, instead of the Grand Trunk Pacific Company. It is this kind of spirit that is telling in Western growth. The company erecting the elevator is the same company which built the new or latest addition to the Chateau Frontenac, and Quebecers will not forget the energy of the staff of officials who came on to superintend this work. If they had not displayed that determination to accomplish the completion of this structure on schedule time, Quebec never would have had this ornamental block finished for this season's heavy travel, which was of so much importance to the city of Quebec.

We talked with a resident engineer, whose personal interests demanded his presence elsewhere, rather than remaining in his present office, but he said :

" I have become so interested in this work

11

of making docks, that I want to stay with it until the first steamer takes a load of grain from the new elevator. Then I will take my leave."

"You know," he continued, "it will be something to look back to in the future."

We might mention that the land upon which the Grand Trunk Pacific is constructing their terminals was part of an Indian reservation a few years ago. Its acquisition will tend to build up that city in a westerly direction.

Fort William is certainly the coming city of the two. The atmosphere and appearance of the two places are quite different. We are sorry to say, so, for we know that our opinion will not be agreed to by the citizens of Port Arthur, particularly those who told us what a great city they had, and how it was going to surpass anything ever heard of in the history of city building. But, it lacks the busy street scenes, the fine asphalt roadways, the broad sidewalks of Fort William, and certainly by no means can it boast of such pretty women, for we were told that Fort William won an exciting newspaper beauty contest held a short time ago. We also believe that the grain export trade of the Grand Trunk and the Canadian Pacific Railways alone will help to make it a greater city notwithstanding all Port Arthur's present industrial and railway improvements, but it

12

1. Kaskabeka Falls, near Port Arthur and Fort William, Ont.
2. Tank Elevators, Fort William.

is good to have two cities so close to one another and such good rivals, for it will make them work harder and more energetically for their respective successes, and in the end they will have a joint meeting some day and decide that union is strength and in this move they will probably bring about the dream of both at the present time.

The ground around where the canal docks and elevators are being erected at Fort William is of a very soft red clay. When we realized what the weight of an elevator and its contents of three million eight hundred thousands bushels of wheat would be we naturally enquired as to its foundation. We were told that in laying the foundation of this great storage plant, 14,000—60 foot tamarack piles were driven to solid rock before the foundation proper—which consisted of six feet of reinforced concrete and steel, was laid. Over three million feet of lumber had been used in the construction of this plant, but completed it stands absolutely fireproof.

The plant is capable of unloading twenty cars of grain at one time, and loading two large vessels at the same time. It will require 135 men to operate it when working full, and has cost $1,250,000 to date.

Over sixty thousand barrels of cement were used, and as this material is now found to be the most serviceable and best adapted for holding wheat, one may contemplate the enormous consumption of cement for such structures in the near future. It is said of some of the old steel constructed elevators that many of their compartments are only used in extreme cases, as they are said to affect the grain if left in them for any length of time.

The ground of the Grand Trunk Pacific Terminals at Fort William being turned into a grain shipping dock and car yards comprised some sixteen hundred acres. Very little material is being lost in the dredging work going on at these terminals, for the soil dredged up is being used in reclaiming some two hundred and fifty-three acres of land on the shores of Lake Superior, which in time will be used for a breakwater as well as a dock for loading vessels.

Mr. Herbert W. Baker, Industrial Commissioner of Fort William, writes us as follows :

" The new grain elevator about completed, of the Grand Trunk Pacific, will ultimately store 10,000,000 bushels of grain. The present building is the first unit, 3,800,000 bushel capacity of the ultimate 10,000,000 bushel capacity. At the present time this elevator is the largest in the world. The Grand Trunk Pacific plans show an enormous storage plant capable of storing 40,000,000 bushels of grain. The ultimate capacity of this great plant is being reached by the construction of units, of which this 3,800,000 bushels is the first and which is practically ready to receive grain to-day. The other units will be added just as rapidly as construction can be carried on."

In order to put down all misrepresentation, misconception, argument, guessing and calculation, the table below of the Terminal Grain Elevator capacity at the head of lake navigation is herewith given as being as near the absolute figure as it is possible to obtain it.

To-day, October 5th, 1909, the storage capacity for Fort William and Port Arthur is as follows :

		Capacity: Bushels.
FORT WILLIAM:		
Canadian Pacific Railway "A"	....	1,250,000
Canadian Pacific Railway "B"	....	500,000
Canadian Pacific Railway "C"	....	1,500,000
Canadian Pacific Railway "D"	....	3,500,000
Canadian Pacific Railway "E"	....	2,500,000
Empire	....	1,750,000
Ogilvies	....	1,250,000
Consolidated	....	1,700,000
Western	....	960,000
Smith & Davidson (hospital)	....	80,000
Black & Muirhead (hospital)	....	150,000
Grand Trunk Pacific (1st unit)	....	3,800,000
		18,940,000
PORT ARTHUR:		
Canadian Northern Railway "A"	....	3,500,000
Canadian Northern Railway "B"	....	3,500,000
Kings (hospital)	....	800,000
Thunder Bay	....	1,750,000
		9,550,000
Grand total storage	....	28,490,000

15

CHAPTER III

Port Arthur to Winnipeg

WE WERE due to leave Port Arthur at 6.20 p.m., Western time, which is 5.20 p.m. according to standard Eastern time. The time changes at Port Arthur, but the city, as well as Fort William, has a law of its own on this question.

In summer they adopt Eastern time and get up an hour earlier, and in the winter adopt Western time and sleep an hour longer. We had Eastern time and our train left on Western time, which was 6.20 p.m., thus we had to leave at 5.20 p.m., to catch the 6.20 p.m. train. This consisted of eight crowded coaches, the passengers being principally women, although there was one car crowded with workmen, with the doors at either end locked and guards stationed to see that they did not break the locks. We thought that they were part of the great army of harvesting laborers going West, but afterwards learned that they were railway laborers being carried to some stations up North on the Canadian Northern Railway, and owing to the scarcity of labor the Company took no chances as it had done on a previous occasion when only two men out of a hundred arrived at their destination, all the others having been inveig-

17

led off the train at various points by farmers and others requiring help. No doubt the two that were left were not worth having or they, also, would have been offered something more than the railway hire to leave the car. The laborer at harvesting time has it pretty much his own way.

The Canadian Northern Railway train upon which we travelled to Winnipeg, was well equipped, the dining car being exceptionally so. In fact, we were surprised at the service and what was served. We enjoyed dinner and breakfast on board as the best two meals since leaving Quebec. The overcrowded state of the " Harmonia ", and the independence of the colored staff, made it almost impossible to enjoy a meal on that steamer, even as excellent as they were.

We travelled for miles along the Kaya-beeka River, a small stream similar to many in this district, slightly colored, and no less impure. It is a wooded country, the trees low sized, and in some places only shrub. We were told that the land in this vicinity was not good for agriculture, but consider-able lumbering would be done when the largest pulp mill in the world was com-pleted in the midst of this lonely looking district.

As we crossed the Rainy River about mid-night, and tried to get a glimpse of Bear's Pass in the midst of an electric storm, we

18

recalled our trip through this district some fifteen years ago, when we helped to unload a small scow of deals which our small steamer had towed up to this point while on its way to Mine Centre, then in the glory of its zenith as the greatest mining city in the Lake of the Woods district. We were the only passenger on that boat the privilege of which allowed us to eat with the crew, so when it came to a little extra work we took a hand in it for exercise and to pass the time away. We asked our captain what the lumber was for, as the spot was fully fifty miles from anything like civilization.

"Oh," remarked the hardened Northern navigator, "it's for some darned fool who thinks a railway is going to pass along here some day."

This was fifteen years ago, and we had now come over that very railway, and naturally we wanted to see Bear's Pass which was one of the stations upon this road. The building for which we had assisted in carrying the lumber, was to be a boarding house, but the pitch black darkness of the night and the fearful storm raging at the time prevented our being able to gratify our wish to see it.

Fort Frances we also remembered. At that time it consisted of a Hudson Bay Post and one or two other houses, including a very good boarding house in which we passed a comfortable night. Across the river were a few

19

wooden shacks, the begining of a village on the American side, for the river marked the border line. A sign (we think) the " Rainy River Herald ", was painted on one of the shacks. We entered the place and saw an old man setting type.

There was a table and a chair, and of course a few exchanges lying about, also a lot of desk truck, only familiar to the journalist. We asked for the proprietor or editor, but to all our questions we received a blank look from the compositor. There was a crazy press about ready to fall to pieces. There was just one rickety case, and the old man was engaged in the process of slow hand composition. We moved near him, and when we attempted to read his " copy " he got up from the stool he was sitting upon, and walked slowly towards the table, and wrote upon a piece of paper which he handed to us. It read :

" I am the proprietor, editor, reporter, compositor and pressman. I also deliver all my papers, but regret to say that I am deaf and dumb—very sorry—good bye. "

We were sorry, and left our card after bidding him adieu, but could not help thinking over this sad incident while we were rowed back to the Canadian side. Later we found out that the old man was no more deaf and dumb than we were, but that it was one of his oddities not to want to talk to visitors. We also passed this place at night, so could not look up the old Herald which, for all we know, may be housed in a very comfortable and modern building.

The next morning, bright and early we descended from our upper berth and welcomed a beautiful, clear, sunshiny day. We were still travelling through an unsettled country, and we could not help realizing what the Canadian Northern Railway was doing for the West, as well as the other railways over which we will travel before we return East. Here we had been travelling all night, a distance of over four hundred miles, principally through an uninhabited district. It is true the train was crowded, but that would not pay to keep up a good service. This however, is not the important point in the building of this road. This route is the Canadian Northern Railway's great grain outlet. Millions of bushels and thousands of cars are shortly to strain the whole system for several months. This grain traffic means millions to the farmers and ranchers, who are now living further along this railway, which, with its connections, reaches over fifteen hundred miles northwest to Edmonton and Prince Albert, and over a large area taps some of the finest wheat lands.

As a man said to us in Winnipeg, "The railways are not sparing in laying rails anywhere, and in all directions, to assist the farmers and to open up new land for new comers. They are not over particular about the building of the lines, knowing that in time they will improve them, but as long as a farmer can solve the transportation question, he is satisfied."

Nearing Winnipeg, we came across such stations as Marchand, La Broguerie, Giroux, Ste. Anne, Dufresne, Lorette, Navin.

Winnipeg loomed up before us in the shape of tall greyish brick buildings, bordering on fine white asphalt laid streets and boulevards. We passed the large Union Station, of the Grand Trunk Pacific, and Canadian Northern in the course of erection ; we could also see the steel skeleton of a thirteen story building, also the fine tall building of the Union Bank, and as we looked at the latter, we could not help thinking that our native city had done something for the upbuilding of Winnipeg, for it is, and will be for some time to come, one of the most pretentious bank buildings in the West.

We were not long in finding the Royal Alexandra Hotel with the aid of an excellent electric street railway. On entering the hotel we were met, quite accidentally, but none the less pleasantly by Mr. and Mrs. Hayter Reed, then by Mr. Kurth, the efficient, courteous manager, who is well known to Quebecers, having resided in the ancient capital for several years. We last knew Mr. Kurth as steward

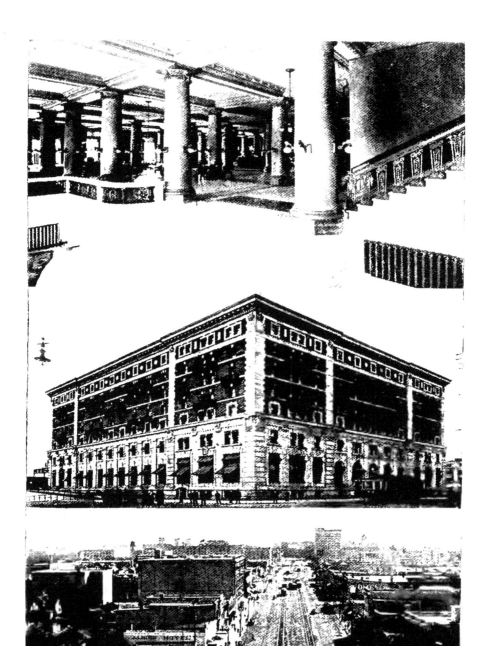

1. Rotunda, Royal Alexandra Hotel (C. P. R.), Winnipeg, Man.
2. Royal Alexandra Hotel, Winnipeg, Man.
3. Main Street, Winnipeg, Man.

and assistant manager of the Chateau Frontenac, but this time he was manager of one of the greatest hotels in the West. We were glad to see such rapid advancement and appreciation of loyal services, which is only another evidence of the policy of the Canadian Pacific Railway in rewarding its employees.

The rotunda of the Royal Alexandra is probably the most imposing part of the hotel, and yet most cosey and comfortable. While it occupies a very large portion of the first floor, the divisions of the several very necessary adjuncts, such as the office, telephone boxes, news stand, tea rooms, etc., are so well devised that the rotunda with its massive columns retains its dignity. It is the half way house between the East and the West, and almost everybody stops off at the Alexandra for a day or two, either coming from or going to the coast. It is now looked upon as one of the pleasant breaks on the trip across the continent.

The British Association for the Advancement of Science was meeting in Winnipeg, and the hotel was more than crowded, but as we registered we heard someone behind us say that there was just one room left for us. It was the manager seeing to the comfort of the guests arriving at the time, and that all were receiving attention.

While the Royal Alexandra is architecturally different from any of the other hotels, it is a C. P. R. hotel and that is sufficient to make any Easterner feel happy and quite at home. We could not help thinking what a good scheme this railway hotel system is. In England and Europe we only considered the railway hotels a convenience for railway travellers, but on arriving at the Royal Alexandra, after several days travelling in the train, we realized that there was one other greater and better reason. Although fifteen hundred miles away from Quebec we were still at home.

As to the high prices of the West. Such reports are all exaggerated. Our day's stop off at Winnipeg was full of surprises in this respect. We paid the ordinary prices for almost everything we wanted, while we saw store windows crowded with many staple household commodities at prices very much below what they can be obtained for at some places in the East. Liquid refreshments and eatables were no higher. We saw a better line of fancy shirts and haberdashery selling at lower prices than in Montreal. English made kid gloves were selling at $1.00 per pair, while a range of fine colored shirts were being sold at $1.00. each. We saw a boot store called " The Quebec Boot Store,''' holding a very prominent place on the main street. We saw a tobacco shop filled with tobacco made by B. Houde & Co., and cigars by Miller & Lockwell, both of Quebec, and

24

in one of the largest general dry goods stores we asked one of the young ladies in the corset department whether they sold the D & A Corsets ?

" Why, " she said, " they're all D & A. "

We accidentally met a commercial traveller selling shoes several hundred miles north of Winnipeg. We asked him whether he knew any of the shoe manufacturers in Quebec ?

He replied, " Well I ought to, as I am travelling for one of them "

We thought that probably he was lost so far up in the north, but he said : " Not exactly, I happen to be only one of the five who cover the West for the same firm. "

We found Quebecers interested in a number of lines of business in Winnipeg, many of them in the wholesale business districts, but we were more than pleased to notice Quebec goods being sold in Winnipeg and other places in the West by our Quebec manufacturers, which goes to prove the fact that Quebec could be made a greater manufacturing centre if her manufacturers would only push the sale of their goods in Canada's rapidly growing Western country.

25

1. Station on Canadian Northern Ry.
2. Kamsack.
3. Starting a Town.

CHAPTER IV

Winnipeg to Edmonton

WE LEFT Winnipeg Saturday evening for Edmonton, a distance of eight hundred miles due northwest. We again found ourselves in a crowded train, and again found the largest proportion of travellers composed of women and children. It then dawned upon us that probably all the available men were working on the farms, or in the fields at the harvest crop. We had enjoyed excellent meals at the Royal Alexandra, which has a restaurant and grill room both of which have a service that would be difficult to surpass, but we were glad to find the same dining car (No. 52) as that on which we had enjoyed our two meals on the previous journey, and that it was to accompany us to Edmonton.

The Canadian Northern Railway has adopted a new system of numbering their dining cars instead of christening them with unpronounceable Indian names.

Among the staff of the dining car No. 52 was a waiter who formed part of the first contingent of English waiters brought out to this country by the Chateau Frontenac. This piece of news may interest some Quebecers who often wonder where the English waiters drift to after leaving Quebec. It may be mentioned that they are to be found scattered among the hotels and dining cars all through the West.

Sunday morning we awoke after a most refreshing slumber and let up the curtain to have a view of the country. We were over two hundred miles away from Winnipeg. The day was perfect and the sight that met the eye was certainly Western. It was wild in the extreme. We were running through a flat country with little sign of cultivation in any part of it, but the soil was rich, and in time population will come. We stopped at a number of small villages. They could nearly all boast of a " Windsor " or King Edward Hotel. " Chinese restaurants, cafes and pool rooms generally occupied shacks. The church steeple was conspicuous by its absence. We did not see a church for a stretch of several hundred miles. The church services, if any, are generally held in the school houses or in the town hall, if the settlements can boast of either, until sufficient money is subscribed to build a church. Nevertheless, on Sundays, we did not see a man or beast at work anywhere or any freight trains moving. An accident befell our engine at a small place called Kamsack, and delayed us for two hours. We walked through the small cluster of houses constituting this new settlement, and although it was ten o'clock in the morning there were barely any signs

1. Town Building.
2. The Lonely Church.
3. Kamsack—Elevators.

of life stirring anywhere outside a few men grouped around the station house. We heard a piano being played and listened to the strains of "Nearer My God to Thee," but they did not come from a church, as there was none to be seen in the neighborhood.

About noon we passed Peter Verigin's residence. He is the head of the Doukhobors and from the appearance of his fine red brick building he must live in great affluence. My informant on the train said that he is the most exalted ruler of the Doukhobors and wields an absolute influence over this sect, even possessing the authority to levy dues upon his adherents for the support of his dignified and powerful office. Outside of his buildings and the station house there is not much more to the settlement, but we were told that this is the centre of the Doukhobors colony which makes it convenient for the settlement of all internal troubles that have to be brought before Peter's tribunal. We saw a number of these people along the line, and they all appeared to be well dressed, particularly the women, who still adhere to very prominent colors in their attire with a preference for very loud blue or red materials.

Mr. Almer Maude in his book, on the Doukhobors, under the title of "A Peculiar People," says :—"But with all their limitations and deficiencies, with their history for nearly a century before us, one may fairly say of the

Doukhobors that (except in times of external persecution) without any Government founded on force, they have managed their affairs better than their neighbors have done ; with no army or police, they have suffered little from crimes of violence ; and without priest or ministers, they have had more practical religion, and more intelligent guidance for their spiritual life. Without doctors or medicine or bacteriologists, (and though ignorant even of the first principles of ventilation) they have been, on the average, healthier and stronger than most other races. Without political economists, wealth among them has been better distributed, and they have (apart from the effects of persecution) suffered far less from extremes of wealth and poverty. Without lawyers or written laws, they have settled their disputes. Without books they have educated their children to be industrious, useful, peaceable, and God-fearing men and women ; they have instructed them in the tenets of their religion, and taught them to produce the food, clothing and shelter needed for themselves and for others. "

" As a community they are to-day abstainers from alcohol, non-smokers, and, for the most part, vegetarians. The vegetarianism seems to have been strict during the persecution from 1895 to 1898, but to have relaxed in Canada, where some of them

1. Farm Buildings, Carberry, Man.
2. Farm Buildings, Carberry, Man.

are located near lakes or rivers teeming with fish which they catch and eat. "

Four hundred miles out of Winnipeg the scene from the car windows shifted from a patch of territory where one only occasionally saw a large tract of grain bearing land, to a beauitful expanse of country stretching out as far as the eye could reach on either side of the train, covered with cut and standing crops. Here we gazed upon the yellow maize, lying upon enormous limits of undulating land, only broken at intervals with a few lakes or clumps of foliage, which latter must offer a welcome shelter for man and beast from the sun's hot rays in summer time. There were no fences, but a number of houses, much better constructed than those we had seen since leaving Winnipeg. Most of the crops were cut and harvested, but there was still a quantity standing in sheaves and stooks—and yet not a soul did we see in the fields, the Sabbath is so universally observed in this far off Western country. One might be apt to think there would be an exception made to the general rule, where there was so much danger of thousands of dollars worth of grain being destroyed by the unexpected arrival of frost or a heavy downpour of rain. We had two to four degrees of frost during the previous nights, which was a sufficient reason for alarming the farmers and causing them to take advantage

31

of the fine weather while it lasted to harvest their ripened grain. The soil of the country we were passing through was quite different from that we had seen in the morning and since we had left Port Arthur some six hundred miles southeast. In the former instance it was composed of a whitish clay with a heavy mixture of sand ; but now it was a rich black with the evidence of producing much better crops. We also began to see cattle and barns, scattered, it is true, miles apart, but visible nevertheless, and a sign of the inroads of the immigrating procession. We were in the district of ranches, where an individual might own several thousand acres of land, many hundred head of cattle and an insignificant home. Everything visible from the car windows was typically Western Canada—the Western Canada we have heard of ; the land that is startling the world and amazing mankind in foreign countries.

We sat on the steps of the rear platform of our car, which happened to be the end car of the train. Here we looked off for miles in every direction, and the panoramic scene was one never ending picture of grain, standing as it had grown, or sheaved in stooks after it was cut ; no fences, few houses, with an occasional lake or two, to break the monotony, if such a term could be applied, but we do not think it could, for it never seemed to grow monotonous. We do not know why,

1. Threshing outfit off to the wheatfields.
2. Breaking up new wheat lands.
3. The steam plough.

but it doesn't. We sat for two hours and marvelled. We wondered how far the grain fields extended, and then we tried to picture the lives of those first homesteaders, and how they lived before the railroad was built, the change in their lives and how happy they must be in this new land of promise. We compared their prosperous condition with the thousands of starving people we have seen in London and elsewhere, marching in long processions under the banner of " unemployed " and the thousands of more respectable " unemployed ", in the congested cities of continental Europe. What a vast contrasting picture to contemplate ? Certainly, the All Seeing One had made it possible for the care and nourishing of these starving millions, and this should be done without restrictions to the pec- niary conditions of the immigrant so long as he is honestly desirous of working. The drone, the loafer, and the drunkard find no place in the West. It is true there is some drinking, but it is principally indulged in by young men with more money than wisdom. A few seasons of the sowing of wild oats and they awake to the deep shame of an idle dissipated life, and brace up.

There were two young men on our train. They were bank clerks, going West to fill positions in a bank. They boarded the train in a state of intoxication, and before long they were further stimulating by emptying a full bottle of Scotch. They made much of their English birth, holding up the passengers that entered or departed from the second class carriage to ask them if they were not " English " instead of " Canadians ", in a manner that made it unpleasant to those having to pass the blockade. This lasted for about an hour, when the expected arrived in a manner not exactly what the young men were looking for, but what they very properly deserved. The right sort of Canadian came along and it took him about one minute to finish the two unfortunate youths in such manner that they travelled in the second class car for the remainder of the journey, content to be seen by few, and spoken to by none.

We took a number of photographs from the rear platform of our car, but towards the afternoon the Superintendent's car was attached and we were deprived of this advantage. Later in the day we were sent for by the Superintendent, who was sitting in the rear of the car, looking out upon the Saskatchewan River, as we crossed over a bridge, the first we had passed during the whole of that day. Streams, rivers, and even lakes were very scarce throughout the district we had passed through from Port Arthur to this point, with the exception of the Lake of the Woods section.

The Superintendent pointed towards the

1. Old Sod Buildings.
2. Wheat Field and Elevator, Carberry, Man.
3. Fall Oats.

far stretching fields of grain we were passing by and enthusiastically exclaimed :

" We think they are looking fine ". We quite agreed with him.

" Look at that field, " he would suddenly burst out, and we looked. There was a field of stooks as far as the eye reached.

" How far do you suppose we can see ? " we asked.

" Oh ! fully twenty miles," was the reply, and we got lost figuring up how many acres to the mile, how many bushels to the acre, how much per bushel and the average holdings of each farmer, and what his profits would be for this season alone. All we know is that none of the leading farmers made less than $10,000, a very comfortable income for one season.

What amused us most was the intense interest of the Superintendent. He was like a school boy in his outbursts over the changing pictures. The waiter came to ask if he would dine ? " No, " he preferred to wait until dark, when the sight of the grain fields would be shut out from view. He was not through talking of the great harvest and there we sat, the two of us, he, the Superintendent of the railway who had seen many such crops, just as excited and nervous over this year's results as he will be the next and the one after, and as many more, and we, a stranger, enjoying it as a tenderfoot seeing a new country.

35

That afternoon we had sat in the dining car with the waiters looking out upon the sea of golden grain, and we were amazed to see the interest taken by these men, who, like the superintendent, had so many occasions to see it all, yet there they were as deeply interested in picking out the good fields from the bad, the thick from the light, the tall from the short, and so on, talking away as enthusiastically among themselves as though they had a half interest in the crops themselves. This is one of the strong characteristics of the Western people. The crop is the indicator of good or bad times. Everyone is breathlessly waiting for the final results, though thoughts of failure do not discourage the people in the West. There is too much manhood and the open air life moulds an honest and open character, tough and brave enough to face every condition. It is perhaps this noble character of the Westerners that caused them to observe the Sabbath in general obeisance to the Holy Writ, while millions of dollars worth of grain stood in danger of being destroyed in one night by King Frost or ceaseless torrents of rain,

Villages are small and churches few and far between in the new land we were passing through, but the laws of man and those of God were being observed in a stricter sense than we had ever witnessed them before in lands where churches were in larger numbers.

At Battleford, which we reached about nine o'clock, we were pleased to see the smart uniform of the North West Mounted Police, and the still smarter looking chaps who wore them. We could not help thinking what an honor this corps was to Canada, and an example to the world, and what a glory and pride to form part of it. The several members of the Mounted Police who boarded our train,were tall, healthy looking men, evidently on a commission to Edmonton, from the manner in which they made themselves comfortable for the long night's ride. There is no doubt that each member has a feeling that he has to set an example to the Indian, and the whiteman who some times wants to play Indian. The Western lawbreakers, or criminals, live in deadly fear of these guardians of the law and order of the country, because, it is well known, that they never allow an offender to escape their vigilant search, if, he is to be found at all. Nothing daunts them in the fulfilment of their duties in this respect. Their record is an extraordinary one, and a great tribute to the good government of this new land.

We passed another night on the train, and the next morning we arrived in Edmonton, having made up the two hours we lost at Kamsack through the breaking down of our engine, the one accident, or mishap, in our twelve hundred mile run from Port Arthur to the capital of Alberta.

37

1. Rush for Homesteads at Land Office.
2. Jasper Avenue, Edmonton.
3. Laying Track east of Edmonton.

CHAPTER V

Edmonton

"Bringing in the sheaves; bringing in the sheaves,
We shall come rejoicing, bringing in the sheaves."

WE ARRIVED in Edmonton bright and early,
and were welcomed by a clear, cloudless blue
sky. It was the sky we had often read about,
and here it was right over us with a rising
sun, which at that early hour of the morning
pleasantly warmed us up.

We were not long in the city before we
were admiring everything about it, the wide
60 feet streets, not only in the main part
of the town, but everywhere for miles, North,
South, East and West, paved with concrete
or wooden blocks, with boulevard avenues
here and there, but particularly in the residential end of the town, which is known as
the "West End". We saw electric cars of
the "pay as you enter" class, a service of
double tracks almost everywhere, and an
electric lighting system that would vie with
Washington or Paris for brilliant night effect ;
white concrete sidewalks with the name of
all the streets indelibly moulded into them
at the corners to prevent some sign agent
making a fortune out of selling enamel street
signs to the city, then taking good care that

the half of them are destroyed by the next year, as has been done in several cities in the East. On the main street, for a distance of three miles, you could not buy a lot under $300 to $1,500 a running foot, many selling at prices nearer the latter than the former figure. The lots here measure 50 x 125 and are almost universally uniform throughout the city.

Edmonton is to be congratulated upon its civic administration, which seems to have spared no efforts to make the city as attractive as any in the West. They seem to have forgotten very little in their arrangements of things. Even now the city is laid out over an area large enough to accommodate a population of 250,000 people, and what is delightful to the casual visitor passing through, is to note the fact that every citizen religiously believes that this increased population will be realized, not when he is dead, but within a very short time, We believe he is right, and although we were only in the city for a few days, we saw sufficient to warrant this prognostication. Edmonton is almost in the centre of the Province of Alberta. It is more favorably situated than any other city in the province ; it is in the centre of a vast mixed farming district and is being made the railway centre of the Canadian Northern, the Grand Trunk Pacific, and Canadian Pacific

Railways, which will afford it every facility for transporting its immense crops.

Mr. Harrison, the Secretary of the Board of Trade, said to us, "Edmonton adopts families. If a man wants society, we have the gubernatorial residence which will in a measure keep up that end ; if he desires to educate his children, we have the finest schools and a University across the river at Strathcona ; if he wants to give his boys a mechanical training, we have the machine shops of the Canadian Pacific, Grand Trunk Pacific and Canadian Northern Railway ; if he desires them to be pioneers, we have a country seven hundred miles to the North and West, in which to take up lots, while we mine seven hundred tons of lignite coal within the city limits every day, which makes it exceptionally cheap, (about $3.00 per ton) while we manufacture twenty-five million feet of lumber and import seventy-five millions of feet from British Columbia. As a packing centre we have the Swifts of Chicago, with a million dollar plant, and other smaller plants. The former employ some seven hundred men and ship from one to two cars per day, of dressed beef. They expended $750,000 for stock last year. "

" Edmonton district proper is a mixed farming country, good cattle, hogs, sheep and horses being raised with great success and profit. We grow as good wheat as any other

41

section, and also oats, barley, timothy grass, and alfalfa. "

What glowing statements from the Secretary of the Board of Trade ! Yet we can vouch for every statement made, beautiful fields of all the grains mentioned and as fine herds of cattle as could be raised anywhere, and the vegetable growth was nothing less than marvellous.

We told the Secretary that we believed the advertisement we have frequently seen advertising Edmonton as "the most Northern city in Canada," was misleading and calculated to do it harm, because it gave people the impression that the winter climate must necessarily be a cold and rigid one, and Canada is sufficiently maligned on this score. This caused him to say : "Why, I came from Halifax, and I naturally brought my snowshoes, and I have to acknowledge that I have never yet seen sufficient snow to be able to use them. "

This was not the only statement of the kind we had heard, as we met others who had told us similar stories, notwithstanding the fact that we had seen it stated in the papers that the thermometer occasionally registered fifty and sixty below zero, in the months of January and February. Upon the winter condition of Edmonton we made many enquiries, and have come to the conclusion that the cold is one of the most misleading impressions of

North Alberta, and of Edmonton in particular, as we were informed by a lumber merchant that he only wore his fur cap twice last winter and used his sleighs once, although he hauls timber every day during the winter. This, and the fact that most of the city men wear their felt hats throughout the winter months, force us to deny that it is severely cold in and around Edmonton, in fact, we do not believe that it is as cold as in Quebec or Montreal.

The cattle of most of the farmers remain outdoors all the winter, only finding shelter under a temporary covering raised over two stooks of hay, or straw and boarded in on one side. Under this frail shelter they rest during a storm and at night. We heard of a farmer from Ontario who erected beautiful barns as they do in the East, but he had ill success with his cattle, which were sick almost all the season, and he had to finally adopt the customs of the country and leave them in the open. The Western cattle will not thrive indoors. This accounts for the absence of large barns throughout the West.

We believe that Edmonton has some inclement weather ; it has considerable rain in May and June which makes it very disagreeable, but other parts of the Dominion have their share of such weather. But we doubt whether any other part of Canada can put up such fine weather as it has during August,

September and October, for we were told that
the samples which we had during our three
days' visit was the natural weather for these
three months' It is clear and bracing, with
a sky without a cloud, beautiful sunshiny
atmosphere that makes you breathe a blessing with every inhalation. No wonder these
Westerners were rejoicing at the bringing in
of the sheaves, for we drove miles into the
country, and in every direction the farmer
and his scores of assistants, were all busily
engaged bringing in the golden wheat, which
was to bring them golden dollars at the elevators. Only one sad feature marred that
drive, and it was the wanton waste and loss
of grain we saw in every direction. Whether
it was caused by carelessness or lack of labor
we cannot say, but it was there just the same
and we felt sorry. Then again through spe-
culative purposes, the land for several miles
around Edmonton is held " on spec " when
it could be turned to such good account.
One can easily see that Edmonton wastes
over a million dollars in this way, but it will
be a long time before real thrift and economy
are practised in this new born country.
Strathcona is a town of five thousand population, lying on the banks of the Saskatchewan, across the river from Edmonton, and
there is, or was, considerable rivalry between
the two cities. The Canadian Pacific built
up the former, while the Canadian Northern

and Grand Trunk Railway did much for the latter city, but in the race, Edmonton has gone so far ahead of Strathcona, that the latter is hopelessly knocked out by political and natural circumstances which it could not control. Notwithstanding this, it is putting up a big fight, and the object lesson to be learned from this fight is well worth being studied by many other towns.

1. In the "Shack" District, Edmonton.
2. A Poor Squatter's "Shack", Edmonton.
3. A Comfortable Squatter's Shack, Edmonton.

CHAPTER VI

Edmonton

REAL ESTATE in Edmonton is fabulously
high to our minds. If you say so to any person living there, he will inform you, " that
he too thought the same thing when he came
to the town three or four years ago ". Many
such individuals acknowledge the error of their
pessimistic views, especially when they make
comparisons, or give examples of hundreds
of cases where property has risen in value,
many hundred per cent., during their short
residence in the city. However, in one instance we could not help drawing the attention
of one enthusiastic Edmontonian to the fact
that most of the real estate men in Edmonton,
or owners of land, seem to value their lots in
the business portion of the city by the first
sale in their block, which possibly might have
been to a bank, the Government, or the city
for a school or other civic buildings, and in
each of these cases the prices were record
ones and established a rate for the remainder
of the real estate in close proximity. Fifty
thousand to one hundred thousand dollars
for a lot 50 x 125 on Jasper Avenue seems a
large sum of money to be paid for land in a
city of the present population of Edmonton,
and yet many of the banks and other large

institutions of that nature were paying these prices. Residential lots were also in great demand, and selling at very large figures, ranging from ten to twenty thousand dollars. We are under the impression that since the establishment of the street railway and the appearance of sky scrapers that the price of real estate in the centre of the city will have to lower considerably, or, otherwise, the important commercial district will move West or North where the properties are more reasonable in value. Edmonton may run to sky-scrapers, and if it does there is room for one hundred thousand people without it extending very much farther than its main street, which is largely made up of low wooden one storey buildings, pretexts if you will for covering the property to realize money to pay taxes, while the property is being held for sale at a very large figure.

The result of all this high priced real estate will lead to the building up of Strathcona which is to-day being advised by its councillors to keep their lots and rents within reasonable prices to attract the people from Edmonton. Time will tell how this scheme will work out, but, it is nevertheless interesting to Easterners to see the strong rivalry of each town to outdo its rival in every possible way. When the many natural and other conditions of the city of Quebec are taken into consideration, the lost opportunities for making that city one of the foremost in the Province of Quebec, must strongly appeal to the Quebecer as he travels through the West. The Ancient Capital seems to have been endowed with such natural advantages that it did not seen necessary for manufacturers to exert themselves to any great extent to keep up their business, and in this manner the commerce of the City of Quebec, which promised so much for that town years ago, was allowed to drift away to other cities, whose citizens lost no opportunity to exert themselves for the upbuilding of their respective towns.

As to the prices of eatables. In Edmonton and Strathcona it may be said that after looking over the list of prices of ordinary household food supplies, we found that they were not only plentiful, but quite reasonable. Rents are naturally high in the West because land and labor are naturally high.

The electric light and telephone are controlled by the city and have been built at a minimum cost. Both are very cheap, much more so than in Eastern cities, while the civic administration of things, sanitary and otherwise, would be a credit to any Canadian city. For example, all milk is delivered in individual bottles from dairies which are inspected every month ; bread is delivered in baskets, stray dogs without their owners are immediately picked up and placed in the pound ; the policemen do one good to look at ; the fire brigade's paraphernalia is all of modern make, and red electric lights are placed over fire alarm boxes so that they can be seen at a long distance off at night, which is naturally the most dangerous time for fires. So we could go on enumerating many other things of this nature which would more than surprise our Eastern readers, when we said that this has been done in a Western city barely twenty years old, and with a population not over twenty-five thousand.

The public buildings are not merely temporary structures, but beautiful monuments of architecture, costing hundreds of thousands of dollars, while many private residences have cost thousands of dollars. Everything is fresh and new, and notwithstanding the public buildings, such as schools, colleges, churches, hospitals, etc., are all very spacious they are now overcrowded and extensions are necessary for the rapidly increasing population.

In every section you see a prominent red brick three or four storey building. This is a school ; not an ordinary one, but a most modern up-to-date institution that can hardly be surpassed from any point of view. We visited one of these public schools, and found it, as all others, crowded ; that is to say there were more applications for admission than it could accommodate, although it had ten or twelve large rooms, with a total seating capacity for five hundred pupils.

In this building we found that the boys and girls, while being taught in the same class-room, had separate apartments for clothing, playrooms, etc. Though the windows were kept closed to avoid draughts, the air in each room was changed three to four times per hour ; sanitary drinking fountains were in all the passages, and these fountains should at once be compulsory in every school throughout the Dominion. The innovation is an excellent one, and will save the spreading of many mouth and other diseases which are contracted by school children drinking out of the same vessels. With the sanitary fountains, which are very simple, in operation, you push a small wheel handle on top of an iron hydrant, which allows the water to sprout up in a little three-inch stream from the faucet in the middle, over which the pupils bend and satisfy their thirst. In letting go the pressure on the wheel, the water is automatically turned off. By this means the mouth never comes in contact with any part of the drinking fountain, therefore, there is no danger of contagious diseases spreading among the pupils.

In the basement of this school there are large playrooms for the children, to be used on rainy days, while spacious grounds answer the purpose in fine weather. In the basement of the boys' side of the building is a large room filled with about forty carpenter's work tables. We thought they were used for those boys taking a carpenter's work course, but in this conclusion we were wrong. Our informant said that all the boys in the higher class were compelled to take a course in this room in order to make them handy at odd jobs around the house. What an excellent idea ! and yet we had to go to Edmonton to see it put into force.

On the top floor of the building was a hall large enough to accommodate over five hundred persons, which was utilized as a gymnasium for the daily physical exercises of the children. On one side was an armory filled with rifles, bayonets and other military armaments where the older boys received regular military drill instruction from an efficient expert in the Canadian army. Another ante-chamber was filled with all kinds of Indian clubs, and dumb bells, forming part of the paraphernalia required for the physical exercises. In addition to all these aids for instruction there was a library for the benefit of the pupils.

We saw the children come out at recess. Each class is dismissed separately, the scholars marching in military order down the stairs to a point where the girls walk off in one direction and the boys in another, leaving the building through a separate exit. So much

1. Breaking the Prairie.
2. Reaping a Field of Oats.
3. Steam Thresher at Work.

for the educational institutions of Edmonton, where children of all nationalities are compelled to go to school, until they have reached a certain age.

Everybody talked wheat, while the columns of the daily newspapers of Edmonton, the *Journal* and the *Bulletin*, were full of it, the fact that Alberta would produce a crop of forty-eight million bushels. There was a general rejoicing all round. But this was not the sole topic of conversation. There was another ; it was real estate, the value of properties, the new buildings going up or those projected. The new million dollar Canadian Pacific Railway bridge between Edmonton and Strathcona was the latest subject to engross the people's attention and judging from the manner in which new undertakings were being discussed in the papers, the making of plans and the starting and completion of such works was only a matter of a year or so. There is no dilly-dallying over such things out West. They come up like mushrooms in a night, and as quickly cease to be nine day wonders, for there is generally something else to take their place. This is the West, and the West moves quickly, like the crops ; no time is lost either in cutting them down or harvesting them. Steam harvesters and harvesters drawn by four or five horses work day and night, performing the latter with strong head lights and a new shift of men. Every farmer has such huge fields of golden grain ripening so rapidly in the sun's constant rays that he who hesitates is lost, or at least, the grain is, and that means hundreds of thousands of dollars to the owners.

Every Edmontonian has all kinds of statistics on all subjects concerning the progress of his town, or his province, at his finger tips, such as the rising prices of real estate, the big value of lots in the main centres, or the increased population of the city, and he tells you that Edmonton had four thousand five hundred population fifteen years ago, and to-day it has twenty-five thousand, and he is ready to swear by all the eternal gods that in ten years it will be one hundred and twenty-five thousand, and if you doubt him for a moment, he will refer you to such men as Dan Mann of Mackenzie & Mann, Chas. Hayes, President of the Grand Trunk Pacific, and other leading men of the country, who have made some mention or reference to the wonderful progress made by this most wonderful city of the West.

CHAPTER VII

Edmonton

THE CITIZENS of Edmonton are as courteous and obliging as any population of any city on earth. If you are interested and have time to stop to listen, if they know you are a stranger or a visitor to their town, you will find them the most optimistic people you have ever met in your life. It does you good to hear them talk, and if you come from the East, you long to get a little of this enthusiasm bottled up to send home. It is astonishing how you forget there is an East when you are in the West. You are first interested, then you grow enthusiastic and by the time you have been three days beyond Winnipeg, you are a convert to all their optimism, and you take as much interest in their future welfare as the Mayor, who, as first magistrate, sets the pace. We did not meet the mayor of Edmonton, nor a number of other prominent men, but we were told that we should have met them, and that we missed much by the oversight. But this was not necessary as we had caught the fever quick, and when we left Edmonton we were surprised to find ourselves in possession of a store of information that would beat that of any tenderfoot who ever visited that city. It

55

was worth coming out West to get it and we are doubtful if it will ever leave us.

We met many Easterners in the West, and not a few from Quebec. We spent an hour in the company of Mr. Anderson from Levis, ninety years of age, who arrived in Edmonton in 1882, and may be considered one of the fathers of this city, and if he is not, he has seen it grow up from a Hudson Bay post, in which he first opened his office as a representative of the Ottawa Government, at the personal request of Sir John A. Macdonald, when the present lots, selling at from fifty to one hundred thousand dollars, could be had for the asking. We are glad to say that Mr. Anderson was a keen business man, and after leaving the Government's service, he went into real estate and is to-day one of Edmonton's wealthy and respected citizens. Despite his advanced years he is the picture of good health and clear faculties, particularly for remembering the incidents of his first days in the West, when he roamed the prairies and suffered the hardships of the first comers.

We met another Quebecer, Mr. F. O. Tims, who like Mr. Anderson is an old timer, and knew every foot of land for hundreds of miles round about, and to whom we are indebted for much valuable information and courtesies in seeing the outlying country, We travelled with him for over thirty miles to see the mixed farming and fine farming residences to the north of Edmonton, and from whom we learned that this advanced state of cultivation continued on for thirty to forty miles still further north, east and west. We could see it in one direction, to the far north, and every word of his statement was borne out by such observations. Such were some of our experience in this vast country, and if we have entered into too much detail it is to give a slight idea of one section in the West, for what we saw about Edmonton applies to all other localities or, at least the majority of them.

On the morning of our last day we met another Quebecer, Mr. Pope, son of Mr. Edwin Pope, who had come in from the north where he had driven some registered cattle some several hundred miles, into the Peace River District, where he had located a ranch. We had not time to find out what he had come to town for, but we can guess that his business was in connection with some excellent land proposition which he had selected, and on which he desired to stake another claim. To return home he had to travel a number of miles by train, then over a hundred miles by stage and then another long stretch on the trail. It took him a week to reach Edmonton, but this will only be for a short time as the web of steel will soon stretch northward, through this Peace River Valley, and these first comers will some day find themselves within a reasonable railway ride of what is destined to be the principal city of Northern and Central Alberta.

We met some of the representatives of the Pacific Coal Company, a Quebec enterprise, which is very little known in Edmonton, but one of the local newspapers was so much interested in the news that it considered the information we proffered it as a great " scoop, " though as a matter of fact the representatives of this company have been working in Edmonton, where they have had an office, for some months.

Among the new buildings going up and to cost over seventy-five thousand dollars is a branch office of the Union Bank, whose head office is in the Ancient Capital. It has selected a most desirable location, upon one of the leading commercial arteries of the city. All the principal banks have very fine homes in the West, and the Union is not behind its competiors in this respect. The Edmonton branch is in charge of a Quebecer, or Levisite, in the person of Mr. Jack Anderson.

So we could go on enumerating the different experiences of meeting Quebecers and other Easterners, who are imbued with that same Western optimism, and who have lost all interest in the East, and we do not wonder at this, as we would ourselves, were we residing out there.

We were deeply interested in the conditions of the French Canadians in the West and made many enquiries on this head, as we knew this subject would be of interest to the TELEGRAPH'S readers. We were very glad to find out that they are on the ground floor in many of the real estate propositions in a great many of the Western cities, and many of them are among the most influential and wealthy. We also learned that they were coming from the East in large numbers, and making prosperous and well-to-do farmers, as well as ranchers. It is said that most of them come out West with means, and acquire lots under cultivation. They do not lose their national sentiment in this new country, and their compatriots in the East will be glad to hear that they have a St. Jean Baptiste Society in Edmonton, with over five hundred members, but what is better still, and shows their broad minded spirit in all things for the welfare of this new country, is in the fact that they have a squadron entirely composed of French-Canadians, in the Nineteenth Alberta Cavalry, which is officered by Captain Lessard, Major DeBlois Thibaudeau and Lieut. Ethier, the latter the parish priest of Morinville, who is probably the first French-Canadians priest to take a commission in the Canadian Militia, a fact that Edmonton is quite proud of. In the Alberta Legislature there are also three French-Canadian members, Messrs. P. E. Lessard, who represents Rapon, J. L. Coté, who represents Arthabaska, North, and L. Boudreau, who represents St. Albert. There are also in the city two Catholic churches, two separate school buildings, which are a credit in point of architecture, one of the latter buildings costing in the vicinity of one hundred thousand dollars.

One of the French-Canadian residents of Edmonton, whom we interviewed on the Manitoba school subject, and the settlement made by Sir Wilfrid Laurier, said :

" It is a crying shame that we cannot obtain teachers from the East, in view of the fact that we are paying much larger salaries than are being received in the Province of Quebec. Our minimum salary here in Edmonton is six hundred dollars for women, and seven hundred and fifty dollars for men, the latter figure ranging up as high as fifteen hundred dollars. "

" Furthermore, " said our informant, " although the examinations are somewhat different to those in the East, the school examiners recognize this fact, and are so considerate, that they will invariably allow an Eastern teacher a year in which to qualify. We are naturally interested in these secular schools, as they afford us the opportunity of having our children taught in their native language, which is the natural inclination of any parents of almost any nationality. "

" Foreigners who come to the West, as a rule, live in sections by themselves, and their children naturally play together and are constantly being brought up in their homes to hear nothing but their native language, notwithstanding the fact that they are sent to the English public schools, but the French-Canadians mix with the English speaking element in business to such an extent, that unless the children of French parentage are sent to French schools, or a school where they will have an opportunity of learning their native tongue, they naturally find themselves playing with English children and speaking the English language entirely. "

If one is desirous of studying the future of any country, and it is those who do so, that take advantage of the knowledge thus gained to make fortunes, one very properly asks from what source Edmonton expects to build up a city with a population of one hundred and twenty-five thousand people ?

We have pointed out that the city to-day is laid out for such an increase, but there must be something to bring it about, and to hold such a population when it has grown to that extent.

This is answered by the citizens who point the visitor to the vast lands to the north, particularly in the vicinity of the Peace River Valley, and from all we have heard and seen they are calculating in the right direction. The Edmontonian will sanguinely inform you that if a half million people, and the area in question can accommodate ten times that number, are attracted to this district during the next ten years, Edmonton will derive the entire benefit of their trade, which means the establishment of large wholesale houses and manufacturing plants to Edmonton, Calgary and a great many other rapidly growing cities of the West, and it is safe to say that the prophecies of all authorities, in fact everyone who has an opportunity of seeing this wonderful country, support the contention that the growth of this West will be a far more rapid growth than that of any other new country in the history of the world. There is not the shadow of a doubt that the West of to-day is but a miniature of the West of to-morrow, and whereas a bad crop of a few years ago would have financially embarassed the West, to-day such a thing is almost an impossibility. The great majority of farmers are now well to do, and one or two bad crops would have little effect upon their resources. It would only restrict their expenditure, and possibly assist in making them more thrifty.

It is hard to realize with labor so high and scarce at times, that the manufacturing interests will increase to any great extent, until the districts are more rapidly filled up, and the labor market levels itself to Eastern wages. Where coal and water power are large factors in the manufacture of any article, there is no doubt that the West will make some headway and adapt itself to the manufacturing of such special lines, but where a large amount of labor is engaged, there is not the slighetst idea that the manufacturing interests of the East will be affected for years to come.

Incidentally we may mention a case of successful land speculation out west. Joseph Durant crossed the line from the Southern Republic and arrived in Calgary with his wife, and about forty-five dollars in his pocket, which represented all he had saved out of some mining investments, but his judgment of location was his success. He worked on one of the local newspapers, writing up the crop forecast for 1908, riding many miles on horseback through the country and visiting various district observing conditions and interviewing farmers. He next took up the problem of railway transportation, and the needs of a railway through the district in which he had spent a couple of months, sending over a hundred letters from different parties to his paper, exposing the " pitiable " plight of the farmers, through the lack of transportation facilities. His letters had a very influential effect upon the Alberta Legislature, and during last session they voted in favor of bonusing seventeen hundred miles of railway in the Province, most of which work is now under construction. Durant was wise in his generation, and secured two thousand six hundred acres of land, at ten dollars per acre, in a location, which at the time, was forty-five miles from Calgary, but near where he thought one of the railways would be constructed. His judgment was good, and inside another few months his land will be two and a half miles from the railway, and will be worth from twenty to twenty-five dollars per acre. On this deal alone he will clean up twenty-five thousand dollars. He was ploughing the land at the time we met him, with a steam plough, working day and night at the rate of one thousand acres per month, in order to have a winter crop ready for his purchasers, next spring, who, he maintains, are principally composed of North Dakota Germans, leaving their farms in the States and coming to Canada in large numbers.

We asked him how he got to his farm when it was such a long distance from Calgary ?

"Oh, " he replied, " quite easily. I have a motor car which takes me there in less than one and a half hours. "

1. Herd of Cattle near Calgary.
2. View of Calgary.
3. Flock of Sheep, Calgary.

CHAPTER VIII

Edmonton to Calgary

WE CAN imagine the astonishment which would reign in the Province of Quebec if some farmers came to town in their motor cars. The Arabian Nights fables would be more credulously believed than such real straight facts.

The steam plough which interested us so much in the West, can plow fifty acres in twenty-four hours, and burns up three hundred pounds of coal to the acre, but as coal is found in almost every locality in Alberta, fuel is exceptionally cheap.

We made a number of enquiries relative to the severity of the winter in Edmonton, but could find no evidence to prove that it was colder than in Quebec or Montreal—in fact, not so severe.

When we called upon the Secretary of the Board of Trade of that city we were not alone. We found ourselves among such visitors as Professor Eugène Davenport, Dean of the College of Agriculture of Illinois and Professor Shaw, an expert of the Western States, who was sent to Edmonton by Jas. J. Hill, to gather statistics of this great North land, for the benefit of the American students attending the above college.

We found it rather strange that such authorities should be encouraging Americans to come to Canada, but the Board of Trade Secretary said this was done because the boys attending the college can be advised where to obtain land at $10. per acre, in a country with better conditions than their own, where it is selling at one hundred and sixty dollars This was quite sufficient proof for us to understand Hill's wide awake philosophy. It also expounds a solution for the Easterner's astonishment when reading the figures of the large number of Americans flocking into our West. All we can say in this respect, is that if the Canadians do not take advantage of their heritage we cannot blame the Americans, or foreigners, for doing so. All the Western towns hold out a welcome hand to all homesteaders, irrespective of religion or nationality. They want men, tillers of the soil, men who can and will make good on their land propositions, and once in the West, one gets so imbued with a determination to get on, and there are so many amazing examples all around to encourage the weakest heart, that failure is almost unknown, while encouragement is to be found in every direction, but the one receiving it must be deserving of it. It is no place for drones, or the man who expects the country to give him a living just because he happens to be born on this earth. The drones are driven out. It is

66

not back to the land, but back to the place from whence they came—or starve.

We have said many things about Edmonton in general, but most of what we have said is applicable to the greater part of the Western country. Some districts have, of course, better wheat lands than Northern Alberta, for instance Manitoba and Saskatchewan, but it is not so much our purpose to go into details or point such things out to the Easterners as it is to give them a general pen picture of this rapidly growing country. Many of the incidents and facts which we relate, are, as we have said before, characteristic of most parts, while it is quite within the reach of anyone to obtain almost any information they desire, from the Government, or railway authorities, on any particular subject relative to immigration or crop growing in the West.

On the Way to Calgary

We left Edmonton with much regret, as we would like to have remained longer, but there were other cities and provinces to see, and write about, and we had to hasten on.

The Canadian Pacific Railway runs direct south to Calgary, a distance of one hundred and eight miles, which is performed in seven hours, passing through a very fair wheat growing, or correctly speaking, mixed farming district, with occasional small towns on the way. Our train was crowded and so was every other train we passed on the road. We were quite surprised at the immense travel which is constantly going on in the West, especially when we were aware that it was a season when every man was required on the soil. Two wedding couples boarded our train, which enlivened things at the respective stations where they got on. One of them took refuge in the car we were in, but their friends had placarded their stateroom and decorated their window outside with such signs as " just married " " aren't we sweet, " " she's only nineteen, " etc., while a string of old boots which had followed the bridal party to the station, was nailed to the outside of the car, below where they were sitting. The next couple boarded the train about nine o'clock at night at a typical Western town. The friends of this party made up a most laughable procession while escorting the newly wedded couple along the station platform to their car. The couple found shelter from the shower of rice under an umbrella, while the party of invited guests which followed and which must have been composed of the entire settlement, were all supplied with some noisy instrument from tin cans up to large dinner bells, and the racket from the whole party until we pulled out of the station, was like Bedlam let loose. Outside of the groom and bride, not a man or woman appeared to have on any kind of clean dress or attire. They were all just as they had left the working field, the men in their shirt sleeves with large sombreros (cowboy hats) and top boots. The incident afforded considerable amusement for the passengers who had never seen a Western village matrimonial " send off ".

But the most interesting part of the trip to Calgary was to come later on when we strolled through the second class car, which we always do when sightseeing or endeavoring to study the various characteristics of the people of any country we are visiting.

The first man we met was a Wisconsin farmer who was a victim of heart disease and incapable of doing any heavy work. He had found a lucrative occupation for the summer months in coming up to Canada, buying land which he worked for a season and then selling out to some new comer in the spring. He had made good, and with his profits was speculating in real estate in Edmonton, and to-day holds over twenty-five thousand dollars worth of property in that town, which he had purchased some few years ago for a few hundred dollars. Being in poor health, he found the climate of Northern Canada benefitted him in every way, although he did not feel like giving up farming in the States and bringing his family to Canada.

We also met another interesting character in the person of a half-breed named Joseph Paquet, whose father, Henry Paquet, had originally come from the city of Quebec many years ago, finding employment with the Hudson Bay Company in and around Winnipeg for almost a half century, in which place our newly made acquaintance was born. This descendant of French Canada spoke five Indian languages, besides English and French. He was on his way to Lethbridge to work in the mines there, having harvested his crop on a farm near Edmonton, where he had left his family to look after it during the winter months. He had married an Indian woman, stating that they were the best women in the olden times to withstand the hardships of the country, and adding, that it was all the fashion, in the old days, not only among the French-Canadians, but the Scotch representatives of the Hudson Bay Company as well. While he had relations in Quebec, he had never seen them, for he had never been further East than a few miles out of Winnipeg. He had started on a trip to the Ancient Capital on one occasion, but became so lonesome before be had gone very far that he changed his mind and returned home.

While holding this conversation with the

old timer we met another French-Canadian named Lachapelle from Montreal, who had gone West, to look the country over, and was so impressed with what he had seen that he had secured the lease of a farm, twelve miles out of Edmonton, for twelve hundred dollars per annum, and was on his way home to bring out his family, consisting of a wife and six boys. Lachapelle was more than delighted to meet Paquet, and have an opportunity of talking to someone in his own native language, as he could not speak a word of English, a circumstance which made travelling in the West quite lonely for him.

We also met an American who had been in the lumber business in Edmonton as a broker for the past six months, and who admitted having " cleaned up " (this is the term out West) some three thousand dollars, which he considered exceptionally good owing to the dormant state of the lumber trade during the last season, principally due to a carpenters' strike. He was returning to Portland with his family, due to the ill-health of his wife.

1. Branding Horses.
2. Horse Ranch, Calgary.
3. The Round-up.

CHAPTER IX

Calgary

WE ARRIVED in Calgary at eleven o'clock at night and found a well lighted city. The first sight to impress us was a racing motor car, then several other ordinary cars while not a horse vehicle of any kind was in view. It was curious to walk the streets to our hotel and realize that only a few years ago the greater part of the site of Calgary was nothing more than a prairie waste with Indian trails through it. The town had a very much more Western air about it than Edmonton. The men wore large sombrero hats, riding breeches and leather gaiters. They had a typical western look and action about them, although the buildings and well paved streets did not convey the idea that we were in a city in the midst of ranches. Like Edmonton, the banks seemed to have vied with one another for prominent locations, and the erection of handsome structures, and as there are fifteen branches of Canadian chartered banks within the limits, there were fifteen bank buildings, and we think we passed them all on the way to our hotel about two blocks distant from the station. We also saw signs of a foreign element doing business there, and one sign was quite amusing. It read " Jun Sun, Merchant tailor, ladies and gents suits made to order, etc. " Thus you see the Chinese have entered the tailoring business in Calgary.

Our hotel was not much so far as rooms were concerned, notwithstanding, it was the leading hostelry in the city. This is a remarkable circumstance, as a town advertising itself as Calgary is doing should certainly provide its guests with a modern constructed hotel. However, the service was excellent, particularly in the dining room which was looked after by Japanese waiters. This was the first time that we had ever been waited upon by these foreigners, and we must say that they are adepts in this line, being clean, tidy looking, quiet in their movements, and exceptionally uncommunicative, even among themselves. The cooking was good, and we asked if the chef was also a Jap.

" No, " replied our little dark-eyed Oriental, " he Chinaman, white man assist. "

Calgary has many things which appeal to the visitor, but he must be commercially inclined, as nature has not endowed it with any very wonderful natural charms or places of interest to boast of, and with the prevailing breezes, winds and chinooks, for which it is noted, and the extremely dusty roads in and out of the town during dry weather, much of the pleasure of sight-seeing is diminished, but what Chicago is to the Western

States, Calgary is to Alberta. It is cosmopolitan through and through. It does more
business than Edmonton, as it has more
wholesale houses and manufacturers, railroad
shops, etc., and its population is now estimated at over twenty-five thousand. The bank
clearings are also away ahead of any other
town in Western Canada, outside of Winnipeg.
Its citizens with their modest optimism, tell
us that Calgary will have a hundred thousand
population in six years. If you come in
contact with a sufficient number of Cal-
garyians, you will certainly believe this
statement to be true.

We do not want to worry our readers with
statistics, but we think a few taken from a
small pamphlet issued by the Advertising
Committee of the Board of Trade, of Calgary,
and entitled, "One thousand facts about
Calgary" will not fail to prove interesting,
as well as offer a fair idea of the work performed by its enterprising and progressive population.

It is first of all the centre of fifty million
acres of rich farming, grazing, timber and coal
lands, and holds the largest sale of pure bred
cattle in the world.

In 1908, five thousand three hundred and
forty-six horses, thirty-five thousand, seven
hundred and thirty-four cattle, three thousand one hundred and forty sheep, ten
thousand six hundred and eighty-three hogs,

of a total value of two million four hundred and twenty-nine thousand seven hundred dollars, were exported from the district.

It has three elevators and turns out two hundred thousand bushels of flour in its mills, which have a total capacity of one thousand four hundred and fifty-seven barrels in addition to a large oatmeal and breakfast food factory with a daily capacity of three hundred barrels of cereals.

It has three cold meat storage plants, and one meat packing plant, which has invested five hundred thousand dollars, employs one one hundred and twenty-five men, has a daily capacity of four hundred cattle, two thousand five hundred hogs, and has fifty retail stores throughout the West, with a creamery which manufactures thirty-five thousand pounds of butter annually.

The Provincial Exhibition Co. is expending sixty-thousand dollars in its buildings, and the Canadian Pacific Railway is spending five million dollars to irrigate one million five hundred thousand acres of land east of Calgary, moving twenty-four million seven hundred thousand cubic yards of material from two thousand nine hundred miles of ditches.

The city covers twelve square miles, has three large theatres, three vaudeville houses, twenty-seven churches, five large and three small school buildings, two fine hospitals costing sixty thousand dollars, and one hundred and fifty thousand dollars respectively. Sixteen hotels, two daily newspapers, one of which is edited by an old Quebecer, Mr. Woods, four planing mills, one of which is the most complete in Canada, covering an area of ten acres and employing one hundred and ten men, a Portland cement factory, representing an investment of seven hundred and fifty thousand dollars, and employing one hundred and eighty men, while its City Hall, not quite complete, will cost one hundred and fifty thousand dollars.

The situation of the city is three thousand three hundred and eighty-nine feet above the sea level, in the same latitude as Southampton England, Brussels Belgium, while it is a hundred miles south of St. Petersburg The mean temperature for the last ten years has been as follows :

Spring	36.2
Summer	56.9
Autumn	39.9
Winter	18.5
Mean annual	37.9

The winters have very little snow, and they are greatly moderated by the warm chinook winds from the Pacific, while in 1908 it had two hundred and eighty-five sunny days and eighty cloudy days.

Calgary is the headquarters of the Western

division of the Canadian Pacific Railway, which employs six hundred men with an annual pay roll of over five hundred thousand dollars, with promise of shortly having branches of the Grand Trunk Railway, Canadian Northern, and Northern Pacific.

With glowing statistics such as the above for a city founded in 1882 and incorporated into a town in 1892, what must the future be ?

The city is not so well laid out, and is much more congested than Edmonton, but its real estate commands higher values and many fortunes have been made in the exchanges of real estate.

Like Edmonton its municipal administration controls the lighting and electric railway, and the Government the telephone system, which is not at all to their credit, as we found it one of the worst features of the town. The operators are independent, and you have to submissively content yourself with a connection when it pleases them to give it to you.

As we have said before, Calgary, is cosmopolitan. You see the foreign element on the streets, and in business, and the Indian, the real old timer you have read about, dressed in fancy colored blankets, squaws with papooses on their backs, and bucks with their faces painted, stroll about the streets as carelessly and unnoticed as white

78

men. There is also a large German element, about the only foreigners who attempt to turn the dry arid soil around Calgary into gardens, with pretty plots in front of their houses.

This is how we were interviewed, as we have been in nearly every town we have visited so far, by the ubiquitous reporters, who gave us a sudden shock by asking :

" How is the East ? "

" The East, " we replied, " why, we have had no time to think of it since coming into the West, we are so fully taken up with all we are seeing in the West that we have no time to even revert back to Eastern things. "

We drove around the heights of Calgary, which overlook the valley of the Bow River, and obtained a splendid view of the city, but the land in the vicinity looks sterile, although in every spot where an attempt was made to do some gardening splendid results were obtained, but no one seems to bother about such cultivation. The people have no time just now, but no doubt the day will come when everything will change in this respect, and the surroundings of Calgary will be made to look aesthetic with trees and grass plots. It only seems strange now to the visitors to observe this state of things so close to the city, when millions of acres of the best wheat and farm lands lying to the

79

East, are being rapidly taken up by home-steaders at $18 to $30 per acre.

At the Canadian Pacific Railway Company Colonization Department offices, which present one of the liveliest scenes of activity, the agent in charge informed us that so far this season, they had issued over eight hundred homesteads which were being sold only in one section, known as the Western, of this Railway's irrigation belt, comprising over three million acres. Next year and perhaps for several consecutive years this company will open and sell homesteads in the central section, and when this is filled the Eastern section will be opened up. It may take the next ten years to carry out this programme, but when it is completed and all the land has been sold, it will represent a population of over half a million people, all tillers of the soil, and one may judge what this will mean to Calgary, Alberta, and Canada in general.

Among the Quebecers whom we had the pleasure of meeting in this city were Colonel Belanger, who holds a military position here Mr. Pentland, son of Mr. Charles Pentland, K.C., who is manager of the Union Bank, and Mr. Bender, son of Mr. Bender, of Montmagny, all doing well and thoroughly saturated with Western ideas and progressiveness. It is doubtful if any of them would again return to the East. We found this

1. Irrigation Ditch.
2. Milking by Machinery.
3. Branding Cattle.

feeling evident wherever we met Eastern Canadians. Among the Quebecers residing in Calgary are : Mr. Miquelon, Dr. Rouleau, brother of Judge Rouleau, of Rimouski, Mr. Lucier, of Nicolet, Mr. Labraz, Proprietor of the Palace Hotel, Mr. Charlebois, proprietor of the King Edward Hotel, Mr. Thibeault, proprietor of the Grand Union and Imperial Hotels. Mr. Dusseault, and Mr. Talbot, Civil Engineer.

We asked a number of the above French Canadians if they had any intention of returning to the East, and they all replied in the negative, with a sigh, however, of regret for the friends they had left at home. We were more particular in questioning the French Canadians as to their contentment in the West than the English speaking Easterners, because we felt that we had something akin to relationship with these people among whom we have so pleasantly lived for a life time, and particularly for the wrong impression which seems to prevail in and around Quebec on this very subject, and we wish to state right here that the French press, which is guilty of endeavoring to cast seeds of discord on this account, is doing one of the greatest injuries to their fellow countrymen. Nowhere did we find a French Canadian who was not full of regret that more of his compatriots were not taking advantage of the rich heritages which were being allotted to thousands of incoming foreigners.

" Let those papers which are decrying the position of the French Canadians in the West prove their assertions with facts, said one of the above prominent men of Calgary and let French-Canadians in the East demand such proof and they will soon see the underlying cause of it all, which in one word is, politics. "

There are some Eastern papers which will sell their birthright for politics, there are others who will go further and sell their nationality, their religion, in fact their everything for politics, but the man who goes West, whether he be a French or English Canadian will find a country that knows nothing of such polutedness or as we would say in the East, such rottenness. There is no room for it to thrive, or exist. The population and the atmosphere will not stand for it.

1. C. P. R. Banff Hotel, Banff.
2. Bow River Valley, Banff.

CHAPTER X

Calgary to Banff

IT WAS 5.45 o'clock in the afternoon when we made our way to the station at Calgary to take the train to Banff, some eighty miles further West, and what a train it was. There standing on the track was a string of ten cars with a puffing engine as restless and noisy in its panting as a race horse at the starting line waiting for the signal to " go." How we thrilled as we passed through that station crowd, all looking happy and contented, and moving about with an air of freedom, with officials as courteous and polite in directing the traveller where, and what to do in purchasing tickets, or checking luggage. There was no loud slangy talk and elbowing of one another as one might experience under such circumstances in an ordinary American town. There seemed to be a prevailing feeling that the country was so large, that there was room enough in it for all, and there is perhaps no place in the world where a woman is more considered, or chivalrously looked after, than in the Western country. It was delightful to contemplate, these few moments before that long train pulled out of Calgary, that great, big, good natured crowd, well dressed polite and considerate for one another. It was mingled with the uniforms we so dearly love and admire of the North-West Mounted Police ! What a fine lot of men they are ! To see them in the West is worth the trip alone. But the starting bell is heard and the conductor's voice sings out, " All aboard," and with a few handshakes with several Quebecers who had come down to see us off, we left Calgary, the Sirloin city of the commercial West, on our trip through the Rockies. What that means, only those who have crossed the continent can very well realize, but to us the contemplation created a sense of the greatest pleasure.

A few miles west of Calgary we entered the Rocky Mountain Pass, but before we reached it, we saw the towering sentinels prominently standing out in clear, dark grey outline silhouetting the Western sky, making a formidable and picturesque background to the prairie land that deceptively lay between the ragged pinnacles of the first ranges which met our gaze, as we approached nearer and nearer, as it grew darker and darker.

We passed an Indian encampment and a number of Indians, real ones at that, rushed to the top of a foot hill as we passed into the winding entrance of the mountains, and gave us a parting farewell with their gesticulating arms as they stood in perfect line. Perhaps they cheered, but we

84

heard them not amidst the loud and noisy puffing of our large mogul engine as it worked to haul us up a grade. Then we felt that wonderful awfulness of being in the Rockies. It was intense. Not only did we feel it, but everyone around us had the same sensation of being in the presence of one of the most wonderful works of nature. Few of us would ever have had the courage to face the trials and hardships endured by those first corps of railroad engineers who have made it possible for so many thousands of people to behold these stupenduous mountains.

The Three Sisters loomed up in full view, and then we passed them and made a stop. It was to let a freight train, in two sections, of over sixty cars, go by. We stopped again, and here we saw a cement factory, the Exshawe Pacific Cement Company, representing a capital of over a million dollars and built with English money, running at its full capacity to supply the great western demand for cement.

It was nine o'clock when we reached Banff. How the scene impressed us as we sat on the top of a large stage, drawn by four horses, and drove off to the Banff Springs Hotel, one of the C. P. R. series of hotels throughout the West. The road was less than a mile and a half in length, but it passed through the little village of Banff and then wended its way through a beautiful wood and up a winding incline, lighted all the distance with electric lights, finally ending at the Banff Springs Hotel. In the darkness of the night we felt the still cool mountain air, we heard the rushing waters of the Bow River and we felt the presence of those enormous mountains shutting us in from the outside world, and we were serenely happy. It was the Banff of which we had heard so much, and which we had often longed to see, and now it stood before us in all its glory illumined with the rays of a full moon which penetrated the valley and threw its shadows upon the hillside. We were 4,500 feet above the level of the sea and the mountains alongside of us towered up another 5,000 feet and some at a distance, Mt. Aylmer and Ball, even higher.

The hotel is beautifully situated and may be said to command a general view of the surrounding mountains, unsurpassed in panoramic grandeur. The service and cuisine are above the ordinary, while the rooms and public halls are large and airy and the several hundred guests who were accommodated under its roof were being given every attention and comfort. The season was the heaviest in the history of the hotel, and the accommodation had been sorely taxed, but we found excellent lodging, and in the comfortable beds our sleep among the mountains was of the soundest.

1. Corkscrew Drive, Banff, B.C.
2. Maraine Lake, near Laggan, B.C.

The next morning the sun shone on the mountains tops long before it reached us, but it afforded another opportunity of viewing the surrounding panorama in the ever changing color of lights and shadows. To the north we beheld the prettiest scene of all, the deep valley with the Bow River winding its course to the far off Saskatchewan. The waters of this river are clear and crystal looking in their swift course, for all rivers in the West, and particularly in the Rockey Mountains, are turbulent from source to finish. To the right is Mount Arundel, to the left Mount Cascade and in the rear a wall of mountains. How the scene on that bright September morning impressed us ! There was not a large quantity of snow on the mountain tops, but patches could be seen in the crevices. They only signified the coldness which was reigning on the high altitudes and which the mountain climbers have to experience in reaching the crests on their sporting and adventuresome journeys, for Banff has become a very popular resort for members of the Alpine Club who have erected a very commodious and cozy Club House as well as an observatory at the top, through which it was discovered that the Chinook and other winds which sweep through the valleys of the Rockies only skirt the mountain tops. So much for science and scientific discoveries.

For the most part the mountains are scraggily wooded, but their crests are all shades of gray with sulphur streaks of yellow, broken in outlines of sharp points and ragged edges, not like the Selkirks which we were to see in a few days, further West, which are flat topped.

The principal pastime of the guests at Banff, outside of feasting upon the mountain scenery, of which one never grows weary, is riding, driving and coaching. There are numerous beautiful mountain drives, the prettiest of which is around Tunnel mountain and to Lake Winnewaka (the haunt of the Devil). The former winds around the mountain sides hundreds of feet above a steep precipice which slightly thrills the visitor as he holds on more securely to the seat straps or iron rungs of his seat. But it was all glorious recreation, restful to the eyes, soothing to the nerves, and stimulating to the system.

There are other hotels in Banff which the public should know of, and they are excellently equipped to accommodate a very large number of guests, while Dr. Brett has just completed a most modern sanitorium for his many patients and next season will turn his large hotel and present sanitorium into a hotel alone. Not only has Banff been favored with a picturesque and health inspiring site, but with an atmosphere pure and balmy, filled with the fragrance of pine and balsam, with the purest crystal water as cold as the icy snows of the mountains can make it, the natural sulphur springs and government baths where thousands have enjoyed the beneficial effects of bathing in these boiling waters. Thousands of rheumatics have found complete relief in these baths, and Dr. Brett's new sanitorium, is most heavily over-taxed. Dr Brett may be said to be one of the veterans of Banff, but we think there is still room for others to follow his good example, and no doubt in time they will.

The dining room of the Banff Springs Hotel is a most charming hall. It commands a magnificent view of the mountains and Bow River Valley, which can be seen to such advantage through its large windows, and as we sat at one of these openings, looking out into the yawning chasm beneath and the giant rocks overhead, we had an inclination to be wafted in some mysterious manner to the tops of the latter. We asked ourselves why ? but could find no response to our query—we just wanted to be there, that was all. Living in the midst of such romantic surroundings awakened a deep feeling of love for those great big mountains. We longed to be camping on them with no other canopy but the stars and the deep blue sky, with branches of fir for our couch and a

89

camp fire to sit around and warm our out-
stretched limbs. We felt something within
us, crying to us to go out and hug those
dear old mountains, live with them, caress
them, and this would be life, the true life,
such life as we had never had before.

Truly if it were not for the ingenious work
of man there would be no Canadian Pacific
Railway, and no hotel to attract us to Banff,
and that was some satisfaction for living
indoors when nature was calling for an outdoor existence. And once there, it is quite
within reach to obtain a tent and pole and
climb and live on the hillsides, or on the
summits of those lofty pyraminds separating
the Prairie Province from their sister States
on the Pacific Coast.

1. Banff.
2. Mount Edith.
3. Lake Minnewaha.

CHAPTER XI

Banff

BANFF IS virtually the gateway to the Government preserve known as the Rocky Mountain and Yoho Park Reservation, consisting of 7,500 square miles, a tract of land seventy miles wide by fifty miles deep. The Canadian Government spends about $50,000 annually in these parks, which grant, or subsidy, is now almost made up by the revenue derived at Banff, Field and Laggan. Mr. H. Douglas is the Commissioner of this closed hunting territory as well as several other new reservations of the same nature to be established along the line of the Canadian Northern and Grand Trunk Pacific Railways, further north. There is no question that the Government's annual grant for improving those parks is money well spent, and if the Easterners could only realize the forthcoming benefits to be derived from this expenditure they would more than double this paltry subsidy. There is a museum and the beginning of a very good zoological garden, both of which are kept in excellent order.

The village of Banff is within the Park, but all cottages and hotels have only 44 year leases with conditions that subject them to the jurisdiction of the Government laws.

The village is well drained and laid out with several pretty avenues, while there are 85 miles of excellent roadways, not to speak of the endless paths along the mountain slopes. Up to a few years ago Banff had only 14 houses, now it has 107, while the number of visitors has increased from 3,000 to 31,000 in 1908, and it is expected that this number will be increased to 75,000 this year.

The Government sulphur baths alone brought in a revenue of $7,000 last year, notwithstanding the charge, which includes a towel and swimming costume, is only 25 cents. But it must not be undertsood that the prices of drugs, photo supplies and such things as the visitor may run short of, are cheap. This is one of the drawbacks of the place and should receive some attention from those who are interested in the commercial welfare of the village. While a stranger may not object to paying ten or twenty per cent increase for anything he may require, he does not feel inclined to be asked from 100 to 300 per cent., and this was our experience in having some films developed.

In making a comparison with the number of visitors who went through the Yellow Stone Park, the Western Government preserve of the United States, we were surprised to learn that the number does not come up to that of the Canadian Park by many thousands, despite the fact the former is many years older.

While it is against the rule of the park to admit motor cars, three of them entered Banff in August last, led by Mr. George Gooderham, M.P.P., who motored all the way from Toronto, making the distance of eighty-one miles from Calgary in eight hours, experiencing numerous difficulties and obstacles in crossing a number of bridgeless rivers. The Government, however, are now opening up a fine roadway and building bridges, not only for the benefit of Canadian motorists from the East, but for Californians and others from the South, so that they may be able to drive, or motor, to Banff, in which case the laws will have to be modified to permit the automobilists to enter the park, without transgressing the existing rules and regulations.

But this is not the most surprising feature of the inroads of civilization into the park. The Commissioner, Mr. Douglas, a few days before our visit received a letter from a well known firm of barristers in Calgary, asking for the terms of lease of 500 feet of space at the top of Mount Cascade, the highest mountains in or around Banff, on which to establish a station for airships. The request evidently had been made by some enterprising foreign company interested in aerial navigation, and this fact proves to the world how aviators are progressing in aerial navigation. No doubt a few years hence we will be able to reach Banff in less than a day. Who can tell ?

You meet the most interesting people from all parts of the world at Banff. You come in contact with them on the drives or around the numerous hotel verandas.

You might be talking to a woman from Hong Kong on one side and another from London on the other (that was our experience) and the next day you might meet a party of Germans or French people, touring the world and stopping off at Banff for a rest. You might enter the charming parlor of the hotel, and find a world famous musician practising upon the piano. He is travelling incog, and not desirous of having his presence known, but his performance at the piano, his rendition of stanzas from Offenbach or Tanhausseur, with perfect technique and artistict touch does not disguise to the few, very few habitues of this beautiful room, that he is a musician of some note. But there is a rotunda in this hotel, with balconies circling it, and here the guests congregate unless, perchance, the night is fine and very warm, and then most of the guests remain out of doors listening to the strains of the hotel orchestra. But to come back to our meeting people in Banff. We had many experiences and love to think

1. Buffalo Herd, Banff, B.C.
2. The Lone Lady of Banff, B.C.
3. Leaving Banff for Coach Drive.

of them as they help to make life interesting while on a western trip, and there are
things that we must say in depicting incidents of an extended journey, and among
them must certainly be a description of
the people we met at Banff. We were
introduced to a lady of culture who interested
us beyond the ordinary. She was tenting
in Banff, alone and unprotected under a
small military tent. We visited her and
peeped into the interior of her modest home,
nomadic looking if you will, but home with
nature, and the foaming rapids of the Bow
river to play a soothing lullaby. Thus our
newly made acquaintance was living the
outdoor life for a return of health and vigor.
To those who have never known the full
visitation of poor health, it is useless to paint
the picture ; to those who have, they will
readily understand that in this young lady,
living her lonely life, we found a noble spirit
full of courage and endurance that had entail-
ed thousands of miles of travel to the most
remote parts of the earth, in an effortless
search for health. But Banff at last supplied
the long looked for goal where a rough
experience of three years upon the prairie
in winter and the mountains in summer had
prepared her to enjoy and make things
worth living for. In this lone lady we found
a friend, both interesting and entertaining.
Alone in her tent she remains until the cold

blasts of winter drive her into a more substantial residence. But she has gained, health, and with health came happiness, and that was the secret of the sweet smile of contentment with which she greets all visitors and acquaintances when they ask her in greatest wonderment, " how can you ever live such a life ? "

There was also humor in many of our acquaintances in Banff. One day we drove to Lake Winnewanka, upon which a small steamer plied up and down the lake a distance of 32 miles. We arrived too late to catch the boat on account of one of our horses going lame on the way, so endeavored to entertain ourselves at a small cottage, the only one on the lake. The occupant was an English ministerial celebate, who had suffered, so we were informed, a saddened life of ill-health, but who had found relief from his severe attacks of asthma, among the mountains of Banff. A brother who was visiting him leased us a boat and was very attentive to the various members of our party. We had occasion to address him several times as Mr. Boatman.

We afterwards learned, to our amusement, that he was a Captain in the Royal Navy and commanded one of England's finest ships. This is one of the many happenings which may occur to the visitor in the West at any turn. At Banff Station we were intro-

duced to Col. M. a near relative of the Nitrate
King of London, England, a man worth
many millions of pounds. The Colonel held
some office around the station of the Canadian Pacific Railway.

In the Government museum at Banff is a
picture of the Rev. R. T. Rundle, the first
Protestant Missionary in the North-West
Territories. The inscription under the picture stated that he reached Edmonton, September, 1841. He was the first white man
of which there is any record to reach the
present site of Banff, camping four or five
weeks at the foot of Cascade Mountain. He
returned to England in 1848.

1. Maple Leaf Room, Chateau Lake Louise.
2. Chateau Lake Louise (C. P. R.)
3. Lake Louise.

CHAPTER XII

Laggan and Lake Louise

WE ALSO met Mrs. Hayter Reed, whose popularity throughout the West is as proverbial as in the East. She arrived at Banff from Field where she had made a trip through the Yoho Valley. Her enthusiasm and ecstasy over the scenery and waterfalls on the way can be better expressed in her assertion to us that : " No one has seen the Rocky Mountains until they have taken this trip." She so enthused over it that we changed our plans and packed up to leave for Laggan and Field early next morning and make the Yoho Valley trip.

We left Banff with a feeling of delight that we had seen it at a time when everything looked its best although we were informed by an American Colonel, who had spent most of the summer with his wife under canvas, among the mountains, that they had only experienced four bad days in July, and two in August. He had returned from a very extended excursion through the country we were destined to visit and he reiterated every word of Mrs. Reed's strong testimony as to the magnificence of the scenery and thrilling experiences to be met with in the Yoho Valley, We saw some 400 photos which the

Colonel had taken on the way. We were fully aware that Lake Louise at Laggan and Emerald Lake at Field, as well as the remainder of the Rockies, including the Kicking Horse Pass and the new corkscrew tunnel were all to play their part in the fascinating attractions to follow in the wake of our new itinerary.

We left Banff at noon on a beautiful day of sunshine. We passed over 34 miles of track following the Bow River for a long stretch of the distance, all the way being hemmed in by giant mountains, one of which interested us more than any others—Mount Castle. It is to be seen north of the railway about half way between Banff and Laggan, its outline being a very fit reason for its christening.

We arrived at Laggan an hour after leaving Banff, driving up a steep mountain side a distance of two and a half miles through a sweet scented pine wood, reaching Lake Louise Chalet, a hotel beautifully situated at the north end of the lake, at an altitude of 5670 feet.

We shall never forget our first view of this lake, with its towering sentinels, Mount Fairview on the left, and Mount Piron and the Beehive on the right, while lying in the deep intervening hollow was Lake Louise Glacier, which seemed to wall in the lake in the most awe inspiring manner. We must explain that a glacier is a deposit of snow

100

1. Bee-Hive Mountain, Lake Louise.
2. Natural Bridge near Field—Crossing the Horses.

and ice accumulating to the depth of hundreds and sometimes thousands of feet which not only covers the tops of several mountain peaks, but fills in the wide range of valleys between the mountains in such a compact manner that the warm weather in summer or the sun's hot rays have little or no effect upon it, and it remains in a congealed state year in and year out accumulating more snow and more ice and getting larger and larger. During the summer these glaciers feed many rivers and lakes with clear, cold, icy water, and the hotter the weather, the larger the streams, while in winter they almost dry up. Some of those glaciers are over a mile in width and thousands of feet in depth. Can you picture one of these huge glaciers of ice and snow scintillating in the sun's rays, and offering the most marvellous coloring during sunsets and sunrises ? No pen or brush of man can paint the picture. We sat with others who had been sitting for hours each day, upon the same large veranda, completely enthralled with the picture, changing in color at every second, reflecting hundreds of tints and shades upon the deep blue waters of the lake which were bluer than any other we had seen, not excepting the Swiss Lakes.

Bridle paths led along the side of the lake and up the mountain slopes to many other interesting points such as Lakes Agnes and

Mirror, known as the "lakes in the clouds," Paradise Valley, the glacier of Mount Victoria, the Saddle Back, Mount Fairview, the Beehive, St. Piron, Niblock, Whyte, the Abbott Pass, O'Hara and Cataract Creek; O'Hara Lake, only recently opened and said to be a worthly rival of Lake Louise, and representing features, so the guide book says, of, "wild Alpine grandeur in its surroundings, that cannot be surpassed."

We did not visit these charming places, but we had the time to ascend Mount Piron and view the "lakes in the clouds," the Beehive and the glacier.

The view of the former and the whole valley East through which we had passed that morning on our way to Laggan, the lakes and the mountains on the other side of Lake Louise, and the Chalet away down several thousand feet below, repaid us for the effort and energy expended in making the ascent, which, by the way, is fairly steep, though visitors desiring to avoid the climb, may be carried to the top upon ponies which take to the hills with no apparent exertion, going up the mountain with as much ease and grace as on a level highway, the riders sometimes offering an amusing spectacle in their efforts to appear comfortable. We saw several men weighing over 225 pounds being carried up this mountain slope in this fashion, and some old ladies, one would never dream

102

1. Sitting Room of C. P. R. Hotel Lake Louise.
2. On the Trail to Lake Louise.

of ever seeing again on horseback let alone climbing up a mountain side, but in the Rockies almost everyone goes pony riding, many who were never in a saddle in their lives, but the experiment is not difficult, as the ponies only walk at a slow pace along the paths. That night at dinner we had an abnormal appetite, which we credited to our afternoon's outing. The meals at the Chalet were everything that could be desired. What is so satisfactory in all the C. P. R. hotels is the certainty of finding sufficiency and excellency of food. You can always rely upon good coffee, tea, bread, rolls and butter, the essentials for a good meal, and with respect to Lake Louise Chalet, the service of the Chinese waiters was all that could be desired or expected, under the circumstances. There is also a pretty tea room in connection with this hotel, which should be seen by the visitors because it is the coziest rendez-vous in the hotel. It is conducted, as every other department of the hotel is, by a number of very well educated young women, who all have some musical accomplishment, and in the evenings entertain the guests by singing or playing. Unfortunately, we arrived one night after, and a night before, one of these entertainments, but we happily were favored with several piano and violin selections in this tea room, while comfortably sitting in a large arm chair in front of a bright log fire. We were not alone in being entertained in this manner for other guests in the parlor overhead were also listening to the rendering of a programme of song, by other members of the musical staff. This is perhaps the first hotel that is conducted almost entirely by women, with Chinese waiters and Japanese bell boys, and it must prove a novelty to the Eastern visitors. This hotel was so overcrowded, that guests, who did not object, slept in a tent, and it was not uncommon to put four or five in a room. The isolated location of the chalet, several miles from the railway station, made it unpleasant to be turned away so every effort was put forth to find room somewhere for the many guests who crowded the place during the present season principally due to the Seattle Fair, as in other years there has been quite sufficient accommodation for all. The ladies who comprise the executive staff of the hotel, were more than over worked.

These were among the questions asked by the guests :

" How high is such and such a mountain ? Where can I obtain a guide ? Where is the drinking room? Is that real ice and snow at the other end of the lake ? etc.," but none caused us so much merriment as that of an old man who in the midst of a rush at the counter asked, " What time does the moon rise ?"

This put us in mind of a lady who got off at Field, where a stop of half an hour is made. She rushed into the office of the hotel and restaurant at that point, and asked, " How far it was to Emerald Lake ?"   " Seven miles," replied the hotel clerk.

" Can I obtain a vehicle to drive me."

" I think so."

" When can I get one ?"

" In about twenty minutes after the train leaves."

" Do you think it is going to rain ?" (There were a few clouds in the sky about this time.)

" I really don't know, but I think not."

" Oh, well, seeing you know so little about the weather hereabouts, I shall continue on my journey to the coast," and with that the lady traveller returned to the train and carried out her threat.

1. Lake in the Clouds, Laggan.
2. Paradise Valley, Laggan.

CHAPTER XIII

Laggan to Field

THE NEXT morning we took our departure
for Field.   We had to rise very early to catch
the train, but we saw the sun rise and once
more Lake Louise was a dream of beauty
to behold.   It confirmed our first opinion of
the night before when we said that there
was a something in its fascination that seemed
to hold one in continuous wonderment and
awe.   The large number of guests who were
leaving by the early train, spent their last
few moments out upon the beautiful lake,
watching the sun's rays upon the mountain
barriers and over the glacier.

It is sometimes interesting to note the
people you are thrown with when travelling.
With us were a couple from New Zealand,
another from Los Angeles, still another from
Manchester, a lady from New York and
another from Australia.   The couple from
New Zealand admitted the beauties of Lake
Louise, but thought their country could
surpass it with higher mountains and more
beautiful foliage.   They had purposely stopped off to make the comparison.   Others
endeavored to compare it with something
else in their own native surroundings, but
all agreed that the Rocky Mountain scenery

on the whole, was certainly grander by far than anything they could boast of at home. We were glad to hear the final verdict for we have seen a few places ourselves, but nothing to equal this.

Our train arrived, the same long train of ten or twelve Pullman, parlor and dining cars which was so characteristic of every train we saw on the Canadian Pacific, testifying to the enormous passenger traffic that was being handled by this Company. This may be better understood when it is known that all the hotels in the West which make money out of the tourist trade, did more business in August of this year than in the whole of last year. Banff was crowded, Lake Louise was taxed to its utmost as well as almost every other hotel along the line, to such an extent, that unless accommodation was arranged far ahead of time it was risky to take chances for securing rooms although we did this in every instance and always managed to find some corner in which to rest.

The railway journey from Laggan to Field took in one of the most interesting and ingenious pieces of railroad construction and mountain tunnelling in the world, and the feat is almost incredible in its achievement. Leaving Laggan we continued to follow the Bow River with the same range of Mountains hemming us in on all sides, with canyons and

1. Yale Pass—Three Rivers—from painting.
2. Summit Lake, near Field.

glaciers appearing at every turn, but of all the mountains we had ever seen we thought Mount Castle, which we passed on the right, was the most picturesque and fully justified its name in every respect. It stands erect and by itself and is distinctively an exceptionally pretty pile of volcanic formation. We passed Mount Stephen, one of the highest peaks in the range, and then took a descent of many thousands of feet into an abyss, or ravine in which nestled Field. Every second of this descent was filled with wonder and amazement beyond description. We made every effort to see how the trick was done, for we had heard of the great stroke of engineering skill on which the Canadian Pacific Railway expended a million and a half dollars in a gigantic tunnel scheme in order to reduce a four per cent grade to one of two per cent. To do this a spiral tunnel had to be built, stretching for several miles around two mountains, and into this our train plunged and wound its way around and around until it had encircled the mountain several times and then came out in the valley beneath. We experienced no undue motion or swaying in the cars to apprise us of the many twists and turns which we must have made in the descent of what is known as the Kicking Horse Pass. This new tunnel road, only opened about ten days before we passed through it, means more than a breathless ride for the tourist ; it will save the company four engines to haul up its heavy passenger and freight trains, which haul will now be performed by two instead, thereby effecting a large saving to the company. But what is the spending of one or two million dollars to the Canadian Pacific Railway? If you take a journey over this line you will see work going on in every section, such as the building of bridges, shortening of main lines, or the erection of hotels, which are costing millions of dollars. Again, while the Canadian Pacific Railway looks forward ,to these additional charges to capital account, as paying investments, they are not afraid to spend considerable money in the exploitation of huge schemes for the betterment of their roadbed to facilitate handling heavy traffic which is increasing in the most astounding manner.

Undoubtedly they have the money to make everything a success, one may say, but it is as easy to make such investments disastrous failures as successes, and were it not for the vigilant surveillance of the heads of the different departments of this great transcontinental railway no such profitable returns could be shown at the annual meetings of the shareholders. The Canadian Pacific Railway know the West better than the Government, or even the Hudson Bay Company. They can estimate the annual crop returns so closely that they are ready for

1. Shoulder of Mount Stephen, near Field, B.C.
2. Field, B.C., showing Mount Stephen.

every demand, whether it be in the handling of large multitudes of travellers, or thousands of tons of freight. Their representatives are as great optimists of the West as are to be found anywhere. Their implicit faith in the future of this country is in a measure the reason for the Canadian Pacific Railway being prepared for a rush, and no one realized this fact better than ourselves, when on this trip and witnessed the hundreds of passenger trains of 20 to 26 cars running in two sections with each car crowded to its capacity, and nowhere did we see these crowds suffering from want of ordinary comforts such as are afforded a traveller making a transcontinental journey. This is certainly saying much for a railway which offers such inducements, and is able to meet any emergency, notwithstanding its immense mileage of steel rails stretching from ocean to ocean, and branching out north and south from the trunk line in every direction where the building of a railway is necessary to accommodate the wants of the people. In connection with freight trains it might be mentioned that we frequently passed some made up of 45 and 50 freight cars, averaging over 30 feet in length, which would make such a train almost a third of a mile long.

On the way we also passed "The Great Divide," where a sparkling stream separates into two smaller streams, the one flowing towards Hudson Bay and the other to the Pacific Ocean.

We arrived at Field about an hour after leaving Laggan. This settlement lies in a charming valley although at an altitude of over 4,000 feet. Near the station platform is Mount Stephen Hotel, a captivating home for the traveller, and what was interesting in the service of the hotel was the variety of nations represented among its help. There were Chinese cooks and Chinese waiters at the lunch counter, whites in the dining room, Japanese bell boys and Hindoos and Italians cleaning up the grounds and track yards which surround the hotel, The Hindoos work very slowly, the Japanese with that same quiet easy manner which makes them, in our minds, the very best hotel attendants in the West.

With Mr. Charles O'Leary, a former Quebecer, and building inspector of the Canadian Pacific Hotels, we drove out to Emerald Lake, seven miles distant, through the most beautiful grove of tall straight spruce trees we had yet seen. This road is known as " Snow Park Avenue," and to the Nort hand South snow-clad mountains can be seen. We arrived at the Chalet on Emerald Lake, an expanse of water which showed up in the bright sunshine in all its glory and coloring, with the frowning peaks of Wafta, Burgess and the Emerald Range casting their reflections upon

the deep greenish waters, a most glorious
sight to behold and one sufficient to stimu-
late the spirits of our party for our expedition
through the Yoho Valley, for that was our
object in leaving the train at Field.

1 Emerald Lake on Yoho Valley Trail.
2. Mount Burgess, from Emerald Lake.

1. C. P. R. Emerald Lake Hotel.
2. Cathedral Peak.

CHAPTER XIV

Yoho Valley Trail

OUR START was made after lunch and our party was composed of six men, a lady, and a guide. As we left the Chalet upon our cayuses, or Indian ponies, some of the men dressed in the popular cowboy costume, others in ordinary every day attire, for several of us had no time to properly outfit for the journey, we must have made an interesting group. We took the trail to the west of the lake, then up a rocky slope, which being our first experience in mountain climbing in the saddle, was a novelty and a succession of surprises as we ascended several thousands feet along a winding trail of loose stones so steep that we doubted that our little horses could ever reach the top as we looked up and saw the distance we had to climb before we reached the final summit. Nevertheless, we got there and as we looked down upon Emerald Lake and the Chalet showing up in miniature in the distance below, and then away off for miles to the East the narrow winding valley through which we had passed that morning, we began to realize the delights of mountain climbing, and the ease with which we were performing it. We were also gaining confidence in our mounts, to such an

115

extent that we were making fast friends and becoming great admirers of that indispensable thoroughbred for outdoor life on the prairie and the mountains. We reached Summit Lake which apparently seemed high enough to obtain a magnificent panoramic view of the surrounding country, but we had not reached our destination, or, the altitude that we were still to attain, for after passing along a thickly wooded trail of several miles of steady climb, we found ourselves enshrouded in a bower of foliage that prevented any further nervous chills from looking down upon the lower plains. But this pleasant sensation was only of an hour's duration, for we struck a trail over a landslide which was our first real experience of anything like daring riding. It was over a mile in width with a trail along its upper edge about a foot wide, at places following abutments or rock ledges, that seemed to suspend us in the air at an altitude of 8,000 feet, over an abyss of broken rock many thousands of feet below, with snow and ice above,. We will never forget that half hour, although not the worst in the trip, but it was the first day out and none of us had ever had any similar experience before. It was time to test the grit of a man, or woman, and at the same time it was a splendid opportunity to gain reliance and confidence in our ponies. The weather had grown quite chilly, but it is probable

116

1. Saddling for the Day's Trail.
2. Our First Night's Camp.
3. Ready for the Yoho Trail.

we found it more so from the experience we were going through. The fording of several streams flowing from the immense glacier above us, was a most marvelous feat to witness. To watch the sure footed little animals beneath us gingerly putting one foot forward and when that was safely located looking around for another solid spot to put the other foot on, until we were safely landed on the opposite bank of the stream, was certainly a breathless and exciting experience for greenhorns. In fording a mountain stream of this nature the ponies made very slow progress while their nervous riders wondered what would happen if a mis-step were made and they were landed in the swift current bounding down the rockslide with a rapidity that would have carried a human being to eternity without a ghost of a chance of rescue. We sat silently through it all, more from fear of the cayuse losing his footing than anything else, for we knew if he did, our chances were slim of reaching the other side of the torrent. If we had known as much of these ponies at first as we did later on, we would not have had a fear for our safety, but then we were only acquiring knowledge and we certainly learned our primary lesson on that first day's ride.

Upon this trail we had several very ticklish moments. We had to go round the outer edge of several ledges of rock which overhung

117

a precipice, three or four thousand feet below us, and in doing this our little ponies had a peculier idea of their own in getting round these hazardous spots, but it was the only safe and sure method. However, while it lasted the moments possibly grew into hours and the perspiration oozed out of our hands as we clutched the pommels of our saddles, for it would have endangered our safety to touch the reins, having been warned on this score by our guide who embellished the advice by recounting several narrow escapes by such thoughtless action. The cayuse are supposed to know more about the trails and how to conduct themselves while on them than their riders, and this we very soon found out. In going around such places as extending rock ledges, these little animals would slacken their gait, even slower than usual, walk out to the nose of the ledge, with their head and fore shoulders over stretching the brink. Here in this extremely uncomfortable position, we would have to remain painfully quiet, while our pony carefully but surely began the turning of the forepart of his body, then the aft, all the while keeping us as far as possible from the mountain side, which we afterwards learned was caused by more of their cunningness. It seems that they do this to avoid rubbing their packs against the rocky surface of the mountain, or scratching the legs of their

118

1. The First Night we Camped on Snow-Clad Mountains.
2. The Author Serving Coffee at Luncheon.
3. Rounding-up Our Ponies—Early Morning.

riders, so that what we thought was a nasty habit on the part of the cayuse of insisting on walking to the outer edge of the trail, was really a blessing in disguise. No doubt expert mountain climbers would have known all these things, but we were only learning and during the experience there were times when the lessons were not the most palatable instruction, but when we got through with the ponies, our training, had turned our first streaks of temporary fear into an enchantment for more such riding, and a confidence in our sure footed quadrupeds to such a degree, that we would have willingly scaled a ladder with them, if they had anything on their hoofs to cling to the rungs. Such is the feeling while mountain climbing in the saddle.

We reached our camp about five o'clock, having travelled a bridle path for most of the afternoon at an elevation of over 8,000 feet. We were thrilled beyond expression with our outing, and the party one and all declared the experience to be the greatest in their lives. At the camp we found a Chinaman cook with an attendant, who made everything most comfortable for our night's repose upon spruce boughs, after enjoying a sumptuous dinner. The ponies were unsaddled, a large cowbell was attached to one, while two or three of the wayward ones were hobbled and then all were let loose on the mountain side to feed as well as they

119

could on the odd grassy patches that were to be found here and there among the boulders and rocky surface of the mountain. The Western pony is never fed on oats and as a rule is never allowed to eat grass on the trail even at noonday when their riders halt for lunch, which seems amazing considering the active work they have to undergo in carrying their human burden up and down inclines that no other horse double their size and strength could ever perform.

Early next morning, when the others were asleep, we scaled the mountain peak in the rear of our camp as far as the ice and snow would in all safety permit, and there sat in wonderment at the surrounding scene of splendour while the sun slowly rose over Mount Stephen. It was one of the sights we will never forget.

As we returned to camp we saw our guide starting out to collect our string of ponies. He was riding upon his favorite black cayuse which he had taken the precaution to tie to a stake near the camp the night before in order to have him handy for his early round-up in the morning. In a half hour he returned with the ponies which had strayed off to a grazing patch several miles away. After partaking of breakfast we were off again on another day's ride through the Yoho Valley.

Our trail led us down the slope of the mountain on which we had camped over night,

1. Resting on the Mountain Trail, Yoho.
2. Ready for the Second Day's Ride.

The Trail we travelled, over 5,000 feet high.

then through a thickly wooded grove of spruce and pine trees measuring over a hundred feet in height and from one and a half to two feet in diameter. We were surprised to see such timber so high up in the mountain and the growth so dense, with thousands of dead trees lying in every direction, some of which almost blocked our trail and yet not a sign of the lumberman's axe.

We reached Twin Lakes, and then Shadow or Heather Lake and here saw an odd effect in the water of more than ordinary interest. In the centre of this expanse of water was a large black spot which contrasted strangly with the bluish tint of the general colour of the lake itself, the cause of the phenomenal difference in the two separate bodies of water being due to a spring in the bed of the lake. Our next interesting sight was Twin Falls, a most remarkable waterfalls of many hundreds of feet in height, coming down through a great gorge in the rock, rushing madly over the precipice and dashing against numerous extending ledges in their drop, until their foaming spray made a sparkling rainbow in the sun's rays. Then we came to a huge gulch, formed by two stupendous walls of rock through which the Twin river frantically rushes with fearful force, creating a thunderous roar that can be heard for miles around, We were hardly ever in any part of the Yoho

121

Valley without hearing the roar of falls on all sides.

We had quite an experience that morning with one of our pack horses which displayed a stubborn resistance to being led by the guide, and on one or more occasions had broken loose from his guiding rope and strayed away. This had happened on level ground where no mishap of any consequence could occur, but while going up a steep incline he refused to follow his lead and again resisted the tow line which was wound round the pommel of the guide's saddle. This caused a severe strain on the rope, with a certainty of the guide's horse and man turning topsy turvy or else the back horse . Judgment was decided in favor of the latter, by the guide letting go the tow line and the pack horse turned a complete somersault, rolling down the hill and narrowly escaping colliding with some of the members of our party following in the rear. Fortunately, the pack horse regained his feet on the hillside, as these ponies invariably do under such circumstances, and escaped with nothing more than a bad shaking up, a sore back, and most of our eatables crushed into a jammed state.

We lunched at a pretty spot in the valley and then visited the Wapta glacier, which defies description it is so beautiful. None of the glaciers we had ever seen could equal

1. Showing Timber Limit.
2. Camp for Lunch, Yoho Trail.

1. Ice Cave, Yoho Glacier.
2. Twin Falls, Yoho Valley.

it and we thought none that we were likely to see could possibly surpass it.

Our next experience was in fording the Twin River, We should mention that all the rivers in the Rocky Mountains are more like rapids than ordinary flowing streams, with swift currents that suggest the danger of being caught in their turbulent course. We had, however, by this time, every confidence in our mounts. We knew they could do the trick, and so they did, although the current carried them down quite a distance while making for the bank on the opposite side.

We then passed the Laughing Falls, and following the Yoho River, we arrived at our camp for the night after a most interesting though long ride of 18 miles, none of us seemingly tired, except our lady companion, who was quite exhausted, but a good supper livened us, and we more than enjoyed an evening around a camp fire, retiring early to rest within hearing of the roar of the Takakaw Falls a short distance away. These falls are over 1,200 feet high with a peculiar roar which seems to vary from time to time in accord with the volume of water which they carry over an immense precipice. There is quite a difference between the morning and evening fall which is caused by the melting of the snow and ice during the day which creates more water for the evening fall, and considerably less in the morning.

Our tent that night was as comfortable as on the previous one, only we slept better and longer, for the mountain air had done its work thoroughly.

1. Yoho Valley.
2. Takakkaw Falls.

CHAPTER XV

Yoho Valley Trail

THE THIRD day was one of sunshine like all the others, and we made a start on the last day's trail, which was to be the most exciting of all, so our guide told us, and as we write now we certainly think it was. We ascended a trail along the Emerald range which never seemed to end, nor did we think some of the inclines could be surmounted by our ponies, but they never failed, even when we were hanging in the balance with a tendency to to go over their haunches. How they had the grit and strength to stick to their job, was one of the startling revelations of our most wonderful trip. But they did, and never once did one of our nine ponies flinch from its task, and no doubt the pack pony never would had it not been led by a tow line, which we believe was the cause of his resentment, though it resulted in an unpleasant finish in his stupid selection of locality for his circus performance. We finally reached the highest trail on the Emerald Range, overlooking the Yoho Valley, and lunched at Summit Lake. Then began the excitement of the day, or, the three days, in following the trail around Mount Wapta, where we again crossed a rockslide, of a much more thrilling nature, than any hitherto, for over, and, much higher than we dared to look, were overhanging ledges of rock, some loose and ready to descend upon us with the least likely reason, The rockslide was over two thousand feet deep and then the slope of the mountain continued on down for several more thousands of feet. Along our narrow path, barely eighteen inches wide, we kept in motion, in single file, as was our accustomed habit, for nowhere, with few exceptions, could we ever find room to travel in any other manner. Away down in the distance lay Emerald Lake and the Chalet. It was thrilling to a degree. The sensation of the moments, the grandeur of the mountain and valley scenery, the magnificent coloring of the mountain peaks, all of which by this time, we could gaze upon without the nervous strain of the first day, was an experience of a lifetime, and we felt proud of ourselves for being able to enjoy every moment of the half hour we spent in passing over this rockslide at places so hazardous that we came to the conclusion our ponies were capable of walking a tight rope if put to it. Nor did we have much fear of going down the slide, or care if the big rocks above us fell from their perches, for we had enjoyed the pastime of hurling these boulders down the mountain side the day before, while looking at the Wapta glacier, and the descent of these large boulders

1. Our party, led by "Bub" Dunsmore, Crossing Burgess Pass.
2. A Steep Drop of 3,000 feet, made our Hair Stand Up.

had given us a pleasure of a rather novel character, for it is not an everyday opportunity to set rocks of a ton or two in weight rolling down a steep precipice of several thousand feet, carrying with them on the way, thousands of others, and raising such a rumpus on the mountain slope that one might think there was an earthquake upheaval

All the afternoon we kept climbing up and up, but all the time there was no obstruction to our view, so that we could see miles away and it all seemed so resplendent and entertaining that when we stopped to rest for a few minutes, before the final climb of Burgess Pass—the critical moment, so we were told, in the whole of our mountain expedition— no one thought of danger, for we felt so good and we were all enjoying the mountains to such an extent. So on we proceeded, going still higher to the peak of Mount Burgess and then around it, and for five minutes there was a deep, dead silence, and our hair may have stood up a little, and our hearts fluttered, but we never knew it. We know we clutched the pommel of our saddle somewhat more firmly than usual, and squeezed the flanks of our pony, as we followed our leader around a point of an extraordinary height on a trail of about nine to twelve inches wide. The abyss was of many thousands of feet, how many we did not even care to guess, for we never glanced down, we simply clung to the saddle and looked straight ahead When we reached a little safer position and found more trail for our ponies to walk on, we congratulated ourselves on our animal's great feat in bringing us safely over the craggy edge without any desire to take advantage of our helpess position by dumping us into the deep ravine below. We had accomplished the most daring feat of our whole journey and the panorama of the sur-rounding mountains, vales, lakes and rivers from our high altitude, was certainly the most thrilling and wonderful of our whole trip. We then made the long descent on a zig-zag trail, winding like a circular staircase, during which time the sensation of sticking to our saddle and doing a balancing act upon the back of our pony, which was invariably walking at an angle of forty-five, was not the least interesting of our experiences. Some of us preferred to walk, but even then we wondered, as we walked before or behind our ponies, how they or we did not fall over one another. In our three days' trip we had grown to love our "Pinto," for that was the name of our cayuse, and we believe he had grown to like us, particularly for the few lumps of sugar we occasionally gave him, which was as many times as we could steal them from our Chink-chink, which in the West, means a Chinaman. On one occa-sion we thought to take a rest while making

1. Snow Peak Avenue, near Emerald Lake.
2. Lake in the Clouds, from painting.

this very steep descent, for we had come to the conclusion that going down such declivities is worse than going up, and it was astonishing to see the manifest interest which " Pinto " took in us. Like the pack horse, he resented being led, so we had to force him ahead of us, but if for any reason we happened to lag a few feet behind he would stop and look around with an enquiring gaze as much as to ask what we were delaying about ; in any case, he would not go on until we got up to him. He paid little attention to the other ponies in the lead, which, considering the fact that he was homeward bound and acquainted with the trail we were following, was to say the least quite reasonably intelligent. He seemed to know that we were coupled together as one part of the little procession of mountain travellers. We have come to the conclusion that the Western pony is the most faithful animal bred to-day, while his shrewdness and knowing intelligence on the trail leads to repeated surprises for the uninitiated.

We arrived at Field at 5.30 o'clock, concluding our pleasurable expedition into the Yoho Valley, a trip never to be forgotten. We reiterate with emphasis Mrs. Hayter Reed's remark to us : " No one has seen the Rocky Mountains until they have made a tour of the Yoho Valley and Burgess Pass."

We left Field in the early morning, finding

the first section of " No. 97 " so crowded that we could not obtain accommodation, we waited to take " No. 5," which was supposed to be following in quick succession. We got on board the next train which came in only to find that it was the second section of " No. 97." It was as long as the previous one and it was filled with Americans going to the Seattle Fair. In the West all trains are known by numbers, and the 24 hour system is used everywhere, which at first is slightly complicated, until you have become accustomed to it.

The same mountain scenery continued on our route as we followed the Kicking Horse River, passing through a valley which divides the Otter Tail and Van Horne Ranges. In the later Mount Goodsir rises to a height of 11,663. Then we descended into the lower Kicking Horse Canyon, where the mountain slopes become vertical, rising thousands of feet and almost overshadowing us from any sunshine, and there one sees the snow and ice on either side of the track. The railway makes an abrupt descent until the Columbia River is reached by which time we had arrived at Golden, where a beautiful view was obtained of the Selkirks rising from " their forest clad bases and lifting their ice crowned heights far into the sky."

Golden is a mining and also a tourist center for taking steamers to view the picturesque scenery of the Columbia river.

1. On the Illecillewaet Glacier.
2. Mitre and Victoria Glacier.
3. Mount Sir Donald and Glacier.

We continued on passing Mount Tupper, Sir Donald, Swiss Peak and more glaciers until we came to the Rogers Pass, named after Major A. B. Rogers who discovered it in 1881, previous to which no human foot had penetrated to the summit of this great central range with its precipices. At Glacier we stopped for lunch.

As we did not have sufficient time to remain over here, we think the following guide book description of this prettily located station is well worth reproducing:

"The station and hotel are within thirty minutes walk of the Illecillewaet Glacier, from which, at the left, Sir Donald (10,388 feet) rises a naked and abrupt pyramid, to a height of a mile and a quarter above the railway. This stately Monolith was named after Sir Donald Smith (Lord Strathcona), one of the chief promoters of the Canadian Pacific Railway. Farther to the left are sharp peaks—Uto, Eagle, Avalanche and Macdonald—second only to Sir Donald, Rogers Pass and the Snowy Hermit Range, the most prominent peaks of which are called the Swiss Peaks, are in full view. Again to the left, at the west end of the Hermit Range, on the south side of Bear Creek, comes Cheops, so named after the Great Pyramid, the tomb of the Pharaoh Shufu (Cheops) who lived 3,700 B. C., and in the foreground and far down among the trees, the Illecille-

131

waet glistens across the valley. Somewhat at the left of Cheops the shoulders of Ross peak are visible over the wooded slope of the Mountain behind the hotel, which is called Abbott. Between Ross and Abbott in the background is an enormous wall of snow. This is the Mount Bonney Glacier. To the right of Ross, between Ross and Cheops, a glimpse is caught of the Cougar Valley where are the wonderful caves of Nakimu (Indian for Grumbling Caves). This is the Asulkan Glacier in the Valley of the Asulkan Creek, a gem of mountain beauty where a series of white cascades foam through vistas of dark spruce and fir, where falls leap from ledges above in clouds of flying spray, and shining open meadows lead the traveller to listen for the tinkle of the Alpine herd. The peaks going from right to left were— Afton, the sharp apex ; the Ramparts, an oblong wall ; the Dome, a rounded rock ; Castor and Pollux, two sharp spires farthest south. To the left of the Asukan Glacier comes a forested dome, Glacier Crest, the Western boundary of the Great Illecillewaet Glacier, which is banked on the other side by the lower slopes of Sir Donald, from whose summit an immense number of glaciers can be seen. The hotel serves not only as a dining station for passing trains, but affords a most delightful stopping place for tourists who wish to hunt, or explore the surrounding mountains or glaciers. The Company has built a large annex to the hotel to accommodate the increasing tourist travel that is not satisfied with the short stop made by train, and this has been recently enlarged. Here in the heart of the Selkirks every comfort and luxury are found, and here many gather annually to spend the summer amidst the wonders of nature. The Illecillewaet Glacier is exactly two miles away, and its slowly receding forefoot with immense crevices of abysmal depth cutting across the crystal surface, is onl a fewy hundred feet above the level of the hotel. Several good trails have been made to it, and its exploration is practicable. A splendid view can be obtained of the Great Glacier from Glacier Crest to the left of the Great Glacier, and 3,000 feet above the hotel. Another view is from the trail at the foot or Sir Donald which is to the right of the ice. Easy trails also lead to Marion Lake ; on Mount Abbott, high among the trees, is Cascade summer house directly above the mountain torrent seen tumbling down the green shoulder from Avalanche Peak ; to the head of the Asulkan Valley, where the ice flow of two main branches of the glacier meet ; and to the summits of Mounts Avalanche and Abbott, Roger's Pass above, and The Loop below, are within an easy walk. A glacial stream has been caught and furnishes foun-

133

tains about the hotel. Game is very abundant throughout these lofty ranges. Their summits are the home of the mountain goat, which are seldom found south of Canada. Bears also are seen frequently in this vicinity."

1. Grape Vines, Kelowna, Okanagan Valley.
2. C. P. R. Steamer on Okanagan Lake.

CHAPTER XVI

The Okanagan Valley

To TRAVEL through the West and not visit the fruit district would be missing a very important section of British Columbia well worth the attention of all Easterners. It is only of late years that it has been realized that lying to the south of the main line of the Canadian Pacific Railway, down the Okanagan Valley, some 250 miles from the Pacific Coast, was a section of country that could produce miscellaneous fruits as fine as any other spot on the North American Continent.

Although in its infancy it can show sufficient evidence to impress one with the certain belief that it is destined to have a great future. The Okanagan Valley is not the only land in British Columbia which is found suitable for fruit culture, as the Southern portion of Vancouver Island, the lower Fraser River Valley, the Thompson River Valley, and the Shuswap Lake districts are well known fruit regions.

We left the train and the main line of the Canadian Pacific Railway at Sicomous Junction, remaining over night at a very comfortable and prettily situated hotel on Lake Shuswap, and recently brought into the corporation of hotels under the management of the Canadian Pacific Railway. From this point we went south some 50 miles to Okanagan Landing, passing on the way a number of small villages, among which was Vernon, where Lord Aberdeen's famous ranch, known as the Coldstream Farm, has made the little town famous as one of the most thriving places in the whole valley.

We passed many excellent orchards and good mixed farming lands in the morning's ride, and at noon boarded the fine passenger and freight stern wheeler "Okanagan" at the head of the lake bearing the same name, which proceeds down the lake shortly after the arrival of the train. We were astonished at the large number of passengers on board, many of whom were fully equipped with fishing rods and guns, for hunting and fishing in this district. The mountains on both sides of the lake are by no means of the same height as those we had seen while passing along the main line of the Canadian Pacific, but are of a rolling nature with plateaus or benches, here and there upon which signs or orchard culture may be plainly seen from the steamer's deck. We got off at Kelowna, about half way down the lake, a comparatively new town of about 1,500 inhabitants, destined to be one of the big fruit shipping points on this lake.

Here we spent Saturday afternoon and

Stack of corn, Kelowna, Okanagan Valley.

Sunday, and had the opportunity of seeing such a surprising fruit and vegetable growth as to make us sit up and wonder at the fertility of the soil, which, to the uninitiated, looked anything but fertile, as the forest growth was but a scattering of pine, spruce and fir trees, growing out of a greyish sandy turf. But with irrigation, this same deceptive appearing soil gives life to apple, plum, prune and pear trees, which almost bend to the ground with their enormous fruit yield, and of a quality that surpasses the expectations of the new comers. Not alone is fruit the sole offering of this arid looking soil, but almost every vegetable known grows here to double the size of which it does anywhere else, We walked through a half acre of ground leased by an Australian pruner, who claimed he had given it very little attention as he " worked out " by the day, and could only give it an odd hour now and again, yet we saw the most shameful waste of melons, cantalopes, squashes, tomatoes, cucumbers, potatoes, turnips and many other garden vegetables of extraordinary size, rotting on the ground.

We asked the owner why he did not gather the ripened vegetables, to which he replied that he had taken all he required and had no place for the remainder. He further remarked that it would be a waste of time picking them up. This is but an example of many other such cases.

There were of course larger and more prosperous orchards and gardens, stretching over many acres, all showing the same healthy culture, whose owners did an export trade to the Territories or Prairie Provinces, which, up to the present afford a market for the larger producers, many of whom are making fortunes. We were further told that the crops this year were suffering from an " off " season, generally one in four, although we could see but slight signs of a dearth of fruit or vegetables in any direction were we had the opportunity of making observations.

The climate of this valley is very favorable for fruit growing, although it is very seldom visited by rains in the summer, but the enormous system of irrigation carried on supplies what nature fails to do, in nurturing the soil. Land under cultivation sells from $150. per acre and upwards.

The town itself is one of the most lethargic of any we visited in the West. We spoke to several of the leading citizens on this point, and they acknowledged that it was quite true, and described the inertia of its citizens to the climate. As an illustration we might mention the fact that we stayed at one of the leading hotels, and while thousands of dollars worth of fruit and vegetables were rotting in the gardens near-by, we seldom saw any of

1. Peachland, Okanagan Lake, B.C.
2. C. P. R. Steamer Aberdeen, Okanagan Lake, B.C.

them on the table, and what we did see, were badly served. No one seemed to care, nor complain, but to the visitor like ourselves who went about the streets or out into the environs, and saw the beautiful fruit hanging upon the trees, particularly apples, which were the size of turnips, it naturally created an appetite for them which we never had the opportunity of satisfying at the table. We were two days at this hotel and never saw a tomato, pear, apple or melon, on the menu. We were served with a large assortment of meats generally with two vegetables, potatoes and corn, badly cooked and served, while fruit only appeared once a day and that was over ripe or green, and then it only consisted of peaches and plums, while on both consecutive mornings of our visit we were served with a small piece of watermelon, about two inches square, a mere apology for fruit. Coming from the prairie towns of the West with so much " go-aheadness," the apathy of Kelowna was killing in the extreme—but as we have said before, the citizens put it all down to the climate, and we have to accept the explanation for what it was worth.

There is quite a colony of Chinese and would you believe it, a Chinatown in Kelowna, and many of the Celestials are working on fruit farms at $1.75 and $2.00 per day, in addition to running laundries, restaurants, and cooking in hotels. We found several of them heavily interested in real estate. One of them was Tom Long. He was a strapping big fellow, the largest Chinaman we had ever seen, weighing over 225 pounds. We met him sitting in front of an ugly two storey wooden shack, on a corner lot, near our hotel, with his midget wife cuddled down by his side. Tom was in the act of cutting a large apple in two when we happened along and drew him into conversation. After we had asked him several questions, he turned the tables on us and said :—

" Where you come from."

We responded, then came the following, dialogue :

" When you come ? "

" Yesterday."

" When you go ? "

" To-morrow."

" What you do ? "

" Write (making a sign with a pencil) on a piece of paper."

" Oh, you lie ? " We presume he meant to say " write," but made a simple slip of word. Then again, perhaps he didn't. He may have done some newspaper work himself in days long ago in his rice fed Empire.

Tom Long owned the corner lot, upon which he was living, and wanted $8,000 for it. He also possessed the opposite corner lot, part of which he had recently disposed of at a handsome price. He had been in

140

Kelowna sixteen years, during which time he had seen the town grow up from a settlement of four houses, and he had not lost the opportunity to seize upon several of the best locations. He also informed us that he only paid $150 for what he was now asking $8,000, and which he expected to get in a short time from some lumber concern who were after it.

1. Summerland, Okanagan Lake, B.C.
2. Orchards, Summerland, B.C.

CHAPTER XVII

Kelowna, B. C.

THERE ARE some very fine residences in Kelowna with the most amazing floral lawns surrounding them.

Among the leading citizens of the town is a Mr. T. W. Stirling, a very large fruit grower and exporter, who had fifteen years' experience of fruit growing in British Columbia, and in the course of an interview with a representative of an English newspaper said that when he came out from Scotland to fruit farm in British Columbia he did not know the difference between a pear tree and an apple tree. When he came out commercial fruit growing in the dry belt had only just been thought of. It was only three years then since the first commercial orchard had been planted, which was about the same period that Lord Aberdeen bought the land for the Coldstream Ranch.

" When you came out to British Columbia, Mr. Stirling, what was the price of fruit growing land ? " asked the newspaper representative.

" I paid $60 an acre for land near the town, Kelowna. It was at that time considered a high price. Further away good irrigated land, could have been bought for $30 per acre."

" What is the average price now ?"

" Good fruit lands, in ten acre blocks, can be had at $150 to $250 per acre according to location. There are unimproved lands with water supply guaranteed. The water is supplied at an annual charge."

" How long is it after planting that an orchard begins to pay ?"

" An orchard should pay expenses in its sixth year. But in the meantime the grower can make a living by growing small fruits, for the orchard trees when first put in occupy only a small portion of the ground. The canneries will buy tomatoes, strawberries, beans and peas. Of course there is not the same margin of profit in growing these small fruits that there is to be got from an orchard in full bearing, but they keep you going while you are waiting for the orchard to mature. The knowledge necessary for the little trees is soon acquired by actual experience."

" If a young man wanted to start life as a fruit grower in British Columbia, would you advise him to buy undeveloped land or land already planted ?"

" He had better buy undeveloped land. If he buys and plants his own trees, he should, by the time they bear have learnt enough to be a capable orchadist. I knew nothing about fruit growing when I started, and had to learn by experience."

" How soon does an orchard bear what may be called a typical crop ? "

" Somewhere about the tenth year there should be a good average crop and your net returns should be about $200 an acre."

" And what is the life of an orchard ? "

" I really don't know. The apple and pear trees planted by the Roman Catholic priests in the days when Kelowna was a mission station here have lasted forty or fifty years, and are still bearing fruit."

Coming back to my imaginary young man who wishes to fruit farm in British Columbia. " Is there still land to be pre-empted in the Okanagan Valley ? "

" There are still some odd lots to be pre-empted, but I don't think they are of the best. All that is first rate has been pre-empted. But only a small proportion has been planted—for instance, there are over 50,000 acres of first class fruit land near Kelowna, and only about 3,000 acres have been planted. The industry is yet in its infancy. The great merit of Okanagan is the evenness of the crops. I have 17 acres in full bearing. The crops from these have been as follows :—In 1903, 120 tons ; 1904, 130, tons ; 1905, 169 tons ; 1906, 172 tons ; 1907, 170 tons ; 1908, 185 tons ; and this year I fully expect another good crop. The value of the crops delivered to the packer works out on an average of $35 a ton."

" Do you find that the orchard lands need much in the way of fertilizers ? "

" I never waited to inquire. I began fertilizing my lands from the first. Of course there are the old trees, 50 years old, that I mentioned just now, bearing fruit without ever being fertilized at all. But you cannot expect trees to continue to crop heavily and regularly unless land is kept well fertilized. The cost of the fertilizer necessary bears a very small proportion to the value of the crops."

" Where do you find a market for your fruit ? "

" In Alberta and the North West generally where there is no fruit grown commercially. At Kelowna we are well served, as far as railway transport is concerned and freights are cheap."

" Do you export any of your fruit ? "

" We have not enough to supply our own market in the Northwest, which takes from the United States about ten or twelve times as much as we can put on the market. No doubt, as time goes on, we shall have a splendid market in Australia for high-priced apples. You see the seasons out there are reversed—November in Australia is like our May—so although the Australian grows fine apples, he needs to import them in November if he desires them out of season. I believe there is an excellent prospect of a market there. The varieties which were first planted in the Okanagan Valley were not suitable for the English market, but latterly varieties that are suitable have been largely planted, and it will not be long before our apples are seen on this market. Although the Okanagan is further north than the rival fruit lands in the United States, we are freer from spring frosts, and when we compete with the Americans we more than hold our own as far as quality goes. At the National Apple Show at Spokane last year, Kelowna carried off thirteen first prizes, and 10 per cent of all the prizes offered, as well as the challenge cup given for the best apple in the show."

" You are not afraid of overstocking the market. "

"No, we cannot grow too much. That is what makes fruit growing such a safe investment. If we have a temporary glut of some fruit the canneries are only too glad to get it. There is a large demand for canned goods. It is impossible for us to grow too much for it ; we can use every scrap."

" Would you advise a young fellow who wished to go in for fruit farming to spend a few months at one of the Agricultural Colleges before beginning ? "

"No, I do not think that is necessary. All he could do in the way of preparing for his new life would be to learn how to handle horses, and that he could learn in a month

147

or two at any Canadian farm. The actual fruit growing had better be learned on the land where the work is done."

" How do you learn the way to get rid of pests ? "

" If anything goes wrong with the fruit that I do not understand I send it to the Central Experimental Farm at Ottawa or to the Board of Horticulture at Victoria. Either of these institutions will tell me all about the evil and how to get rid of it."

" I suppose you are always planting new trees. Where do you get them ? "

" We used to get them mostly from Victoria but now we have nurseries in the valley, and can get locally grown trees which are more satisfactory. The seedlings are imported from France and budded with the varities required. "

The mildness of the Okanagan Valley may be judged by the fact that the Canadian Pacific passenger and freight boats, including car ferries, run the year round, as it is never sufficiently cold to freeze the lake over, or make it uncomfortably chilly for the passengers, though the boats are not in any way prepared to withstand any very low temperature.

On the steamer we met a man with all the characteristics of a real " down East Yankee." In dress, conversation and general appearance, as well as speech and chewing tobacco, he was up to the mark. As he made our acquaintance, he said :—

"Be you looking the country over ?" to which we replied in the affirmative. Then followed a long story of his four years' experience in Canada. He had crossed the line, to the South of us with five grown up sons and a son-in-law. They each took a three-quarter section, totalling up over 2,000 acres of land in the vicinity of Lethbridge, at $10. per acre, and during the first year had over half their property ploughed and seeded, but the old man could not stand the "goll darn cold weather months," and had sold out and bought himself a house, leaving the sons to work out their destiny, as best they could. He argued that it was no country for a white man, with the snow and ice and nothing to do in winter, but sit around the fire, which made him so all fired tired and sick of the whole goll darned business, that he had decided to pull out and "get himself a little place where he could keep a few chickens and cows and them sort of cattle, and have a little more pleasure in his old age."

"Did you make any money while in Canada ?" we ventured to ask.

"Oh, golley yes, sold all my land for $18 an acre, besides, I raised several large crops, but the winter is too goll darn cold for me, I've got to get a warmer climate, and I'm told this here place is about right."

" Then you are not disgusted with Canada and returning home ? " we enquired.

" Oh, gosh darn it, no, not if I can find something around this here valley, which seems to look pretty good so far. Say ! let me tell you something ! " (He pulled out a picture of a comfortable cottage and showed it to us.) " See ! that's mine ! You know I'm a carpenter by trade and I built that during my spare hours. What do you thing of it ? "

" Fine", we remarked.

" Well, that's worth $2,800 not counting the land, I got a good chance to swap it for 17 acres of land at the other end of this here lake, at a place called Penticton and I be going down to see what it looks like, and if it be as good as I am told it is, I guess I'll make the swap and come and live here I can't stand that goll darn cold winter, sitting around doing nothing. You know it kills me. "

This is about the kind of pessimism you meet in the West, if you ever meet any. A man may be tired of one place and sells out and moves to another where he obtains more congenial weather and other amenities in farming or fruit-growing to suit his inclination.

On the way down from the main line of the Canadian Pacific Railway we ran across

150

two old men, looking alike, dressed alike, and talking, and walking alike. You couldn't tell them apart, for they were twin brothers, 72 years old and gray haired. They were returning from Sicamous Junction where they had gone to meet an old Scotch friend, whom they had not seen for fifty years, and, no doubt, they enjoyed the fun of dressing up in every detail, as much like one another to entertain their old friend. We engaged in conversation with them, and asked if fruit farming in the Okanagan Valley paid ?

"Well," replied one of them, "I have ten acres of fruit land, I would not sell for $25,000." Evidently the twin brothers were doing well.

But the land in this valley, or district is not all good. There is a great amount of soil that has too much clay or alkali, and is almost worthless, and this the new-comer has to be on his guard against when purchasing fruit lands.

While at breakfast on the last morning of our stay in Kelowna, our neighbour, at the table, a young Englishman, told us of a case in point, where a friend of his had purchased ten acres making a first payment of $500. He worked on it for a whole year, only to find that the soil was unproductive and he was so disheartened with his first venture in Canada, that he was leaving for Australia.

151

1. Indians gathering hops, Vernon, B.C.
2. Scene near Vernon, B.C.
3. Orchards near Vernon. B.C

CHAPTER XVIII

Vernon, B. C.

WE LEFT Kelowna in the early morn, and arrived at Vernon at noon, where we found a town with more signs of life and " go-aheadness " than any we had seen in the valley. Here we visited the Coldstream farm established by Lord Aberdeen, formerly Governor-General of Canada. It was a marvellous sight to behold ; not hundreds, but thousands of orchard trees laden with fruit, principally apples. This property occupies over ten thousand acres of land, almost all under irrigation, which is the sole secret of its great success. In all this valley, so well adapted by nature, both in soil and climatic conditions, with lakes on the summits of the bordering mountains to provide sufficient water for the artificial process of irrigation, it is startlingly wonderful to think of its undoubted future.

On the Coldstream farm, we found Chinese, Japanese, Hindoos, and Indians, all employed in the gathering of the crop, a veritable army of men, though they seemed too few for the immense crop that was visible in all directions, The Indians, to the number of two hundred, are attracted to this farm every harvest season from the States, coming with their families and camping close to the hop vines, where they are busily engaged in picking hops, making a scene that puts one in mind of the cotton workers in the South, only more picturesque, for the Indian's costumes are bright green, red and blue flannel, and loud colored bandanas tied around their heads. There were old and young, all working alike, for the Coldstream Company at so much per box.

We found Vernon was largely inhabited by a very nice class of people, and in the environs were some handsome houses, occupied by retired Colonels, Majors and Captains of the English Army. We heard of the hardships endured by some of the new comers, who had taken up lands many miles from the town, where they were spending their whole first year in making a horse trail from the main road into their properties. We asked one of these pioneers, a veteran of the South African war, how he expected to make good on his prospects, to which he said : " That during the coming winter he expected to make some money carting fire wood to the town, for which he could get $5. per cord, and with this hard-earned money he would buy and plant some trees next spring. In the meantime, he was growing sufficient vegetables to provide for himself and man, and when he had his trail built, and a shack erected he intended bringing out his wife, who was now in England." This is the type of man who is going to win out, but it was going to cost him the effort of his life. The West is full of such men, and it is such as they who make the West. To those who imagine the first years of construction to be a patch of roses, it is better that they keep clear of Western Canada, but to those who are willing to work under the somewhat trying conditions, the West offers a golden opportunity, such as no other country in the world can offer. There is a something in the air, an atmosphere of encouragement which never says die. There is no past, it is all in the future, and the country swarms with brawny men, who have set the pace, and led the way, and their success is a shining example to others to go and do likewise, and no one with a determination fails.

Everything on the Coldstream farm is measured by tons, they ship tons of apples, tons of tomatoes, tons of onions and tons of hops, plums, etc.

The returns from the orchard bearing lands, amounting to only 200 acres, of the 1,500 acres, were for 1908, over 700 tons.

The natural home markets are to be found in the North West Provinces, and the Pacific Coast cities—Vancouver and Victoria, with an ever-increasing demand as the Provinces increase in population. Shipments have also been made to Australia and England with very satisfactory results.

British Columbia fruit won the gold medal at the Colonial Fruit Exhibitions held in London in 1906–1907 and 1908, and in addition to the colonial varieties the Coldstreams have planted those most in demand on the London market.

To facilitate the marketing of the produce of the district, the Coldstream Valley Fruit Packing Company, Limited, has been formed in which the Coldstream Estate Company, Limited, is largely interested, to equip and operate packing houses at various points in the valley.

By means of this company the small grower is assured of having his output uniformly graded, properly packed and placed on the market in such a condition as to secure the highest price. This is exactly what is required in the more southern districts of the Okanagan Valley.

The Coldstream Company also goes in for the raising of cattle, horses, chickens, and grows a large quantity of hay and oats, for feeding these animals.

The Company has also thirty acres of nurseries in which all the varieties of fruit trees suitable to the district are raised, besides shade and ornamental trees and shrubs. It sells trees to purchasers in any quantity at the current market prices. This

1, 2 and 3. Indians Harvesting Hops on Aberdeen Farm, Vernon.

is considered a distinct gain to the orchardist to have home grown trees.

The nursery stock is grown from the Company's orchard, and the estate has gone through a number of years of orchard culture under the best experts that could be procured from Washington, Oregon and California, the Company being thus in a good position to advise intending purchasers as to the best variety of fruit to plant.

The policy of the Company is to develop a portion of the estate for the purpose of sale. This development consists in applying a system of irrigation, planting with suitable fruit trees, and dividing into lots, ranging from one to twenty acres with the necessary roads. It being essential to have good water the company has installed a system of waterworks, deriving the supply from springs in the neighbourhood and distributing it in pipes. Purchasers are allowed to make connections with the main at the nearest point, with a maintenance charge of one and a half dollars per month for the use of same.

The Company supplies young trees, and undertakes, at the option of the purchaser, to cultivate and generally supervise the growing orchard for one year, and after that period by arrangement for a further term if desired. Charge for this work is based on the actual cost plus a small percentage for management. The only other charges are municipal rates and taxes, which in 1908 amounted to less than one-fifth of one per cent, on the assessed values. Water charges are estimated in a normal year to be $4.00 per acre for fruit ; and any improvements, such as fencing, gates, etc., are erected by the Company for the purchaser at actual cost.

Vernon contains churches of almost all denominations and excellent schools, hospitals and hotels. There is considerable shooting and hunting in the neighborhood, which includes partridges, chicken, ruffed and blue grouse, deer, bear, lynx, panther. Rainbow, and brook trout abound. Further information about this interesting Coldstream farm may be had by addressing the Company at Vernon, which distributes some excellent literature with fine half tone engravings.

We returned to Sicamous Junction, and once more continued our journey on the main line of the Canadian Pacific. While waiting for the train from the East, we met a French-Canadian, formerly from Cap Chatte, named Emond, whose story of life in the West in the early days of the building up of the country, proves that the French-Canadian from the Province of Quebec, played a most important part, and we think that it is up to some writer to bring together the many daring exploits and hardships borne by these people in this Western land. No doubt,

160

the French Missionaries had a great deal to do with this early movement.

Emond's story has some dramatic incidents in it. In substance he said : "On landing in Golden late in August I started to help to build up the town, remaining there for three years. This was before the country was settled as it is to-day. After this I made several expeditions West, until I reached Ascroft, fifty miles below Camp Brooks, on my way to reach the head of Fraser River, but I heard there was eight feet of snow on the trail and so decided to go back to Anderlay in order to prospect in the vicinity for minerals. When I arrived there I found that the whole town had been prospected many years before, and trees were growing in the pits. Being slightly discouraged, I camped with a man named E. L. Fortune, a Scotchman, remaining with him for ten years, assisting him in farming. In 1897 after the excitement of the Cariboo mineral discoveries, I got the fever and started out upon a prospecting journey. By this time I had learned something about the formation of ranges and ledges and with such knowledge managed to find some minerals about twenty miles from Simard, thirty-five miles north of Sicamous. I found there a ledge of minerals, silver, gelina and copper, six feet of good ore for the space of five miles, along which I have claims, but I have great hope of finding

161

many still greater than these in the vicinity."

After his many years of hardships in helping to open up the Great West, with a streak of bad luck in his adventures, he was still hopeful. We saw him descend from the station platform with heavy bags of camp supplies and provisions, and enter a small boat and row away in the quiet twilight at the close of a beautiful day, for a lonely point at the north end of the lake. His last words were "Tell my friends in Quebec, that Emond will strike it rich some day, and then he will go back to see them all again."

1. C. P. Ry. Station, Vancouver, B.C.
2. Hotel Vancouver, B.C.
3. Hastings Street, Vancouver, B.C.

CHAPTER XIX

Sicamous to Vancouver

SICAMOUS JUNCTION is about what its name implies,—a railway junction with a semi-station house and hotel and a long platform at the end of which is a little low building which is Post Office and General Store. At the other end there is another hotel building, no doubt the opposition or overflow house, and it is a good thing there is such a refuge, as many travellers would have to sleep out in the open, as the junction hotel accommodation is much too small, but we understand it is to be enlarged in 1910.

We arrived at about 5 p.m., and a few minutes afterwards in pulled a long train of twelve cars from the East. It remained several minutes, and then continued on to the West. A couple of hours later another train from the East arrived. It was the first section of the train we were going on. In this section there were cars, crowded with Chinese, four of five baggage and mail cars, and one or two first class cars, all crowded. There was an Empress boat leaving for the Orient on the morrow, and the Chinese were from New York and other large centres, on their way home for a short vacation, with their pockets filled with American and Can-

163

adian gold. This train pulled out of the junction, and a few minutes afterwards in came a second section, another long procession of Pullman, dining and sleeping cars, every one of which seemed to be filled to its capacity. It had grown dark, and as we sat on the back of the observation car, generally attached to the rear of all trains of the Canadian Pacific Railway, we looked out in the gloaming, amidst mountains, lakes and valleys. Our train was running at the rate of forty miles an hour, upon ninety pound steel rails, as solid a roadway as a bed of rock could make it. We sat with a group of travellers, who, like ourselves were affected by the sublimity of the scenery. It was a night to set one's imagination at work on all kinds of kaleidoscopic pictures of that great mountain land through which we were journeying in comfort and luxury in such contrast, to the trail of former days, over which, the Indians, fur traders and the missionaries, struggled in hardship.

We were not long in Vancouver, which we reached next morning, without forming the very highest opinion of it. Of all the cities of the West we would have no hesitation in saying that we saw in it a brighter and greater future than in any of the others. There was a solidity about its streets, buildings and its commerce. It was not so conspicuous in deserted streets, high priced lots and discounted land values, as some cities we had seen. A large portion of Vancouver is concrete and set, and business in that centre has an air of regularity about it, that at once impresses the visitor with a belief that he is in a miniature Chicago, St. Paul or some other large Western American town, for it is more American than Canadian in its appearance, and its mode of doing business. There is no harm in making this statement. Even the currency is largely American, and we could never escape carrying those cumbersome silver dollars, which seemed to be passed out to us each time we changed a Canadian five dollar bill. The streets are wide, well paved and the stores universally up-to-date, while the Vancouver hotel, managed by a well known Quebecer, Mr. Charles Derouville, is among the most prosperous of the Canadian Pacific Railway's Western hotels.

Vancouver is full of surprises for the stranger, but none so great as that of its history, its wonderful growth and its enormous building operations and real estate transactions. The city is not twenty-five years old, and yet, it has 100,000 population, and is increasing at the rate of 10,000 per annum, while its real estate sales amount to half a million dollars per diem, fifteen million per month, etc. Its streets are alive, both day and night, while its electrical display, participated in by almost every firm, hotel and public building, makes it a veritable maze of brilliancy after night fall. So enterprising, and progressive, and greater still, believing so ardently in advertising, the merchants of one of Vancouver's business streets, not satisfied with the city's string of electric lights, and the hundreds of individual lights, made up a fund and are paying for thousands of extra lights, which have been festooned across the street, and the effect at night, is certainly attractive as well as dazzling. It is one of the sights of Vancouver to pass along this street.

We saw thirteen storey buildings going up, and hundreds of beautiful residences in the course of erection, not only in one section, but in all directions, and heard of many more about to be begun, while a drive through the residential districts cannot help but astonish the visitor.

Vancouver is as aesthetic in its residential architecture as any city double its size. Almost every house is surrounded with a beautiful lawn, floral bower or hedge, making a varied and changing setting at every turn as one drives through these beautiful streets, where the well to do Vancouverites reside.

But Stanley Park is certainly the most beautiful feature in the city. It occupies acres of the most lordly and stately woodland of British Columbia, situated upon

1. Surf Bathing, English Bay, Vancouver.
2. Big Hollow Cedar, Stanley Park, Vancouver.

an island surrounded by the sea, with nine miles of driveways and twenty-two miles of foot paths laid out in such a manner that the Park is seen to advantage either in vehicles or in walking. The views at different coigns of vantage are most picturesque, and to use the western phrase: " make you sit up and marvel " at the natural inheritance of Canada's western mainland city. It is said that this is the largest park of the kind in the world, and we believe it.

Vancouver has all kinds of conveyances for seeing the city, from a large number of tally-hos, to large observation cars, automobiles and carriages, among the latter some handsome equipages, drawn by pairs of graceful steppers that would look well in Central Park, New York, or at any Eastern horse show, and we understand that both in Vancouver and Victoria, these latter entertainments are no mean affairs in the display of fine thoroughbreds, as well as the handsome gowns of a very aristocratic audience.

Only a few steps from our hotel was the station, the terminal of Canada's great transcontinental railway and nearby the wharf of the Canadian Pacific Railway for its Pacific and Orient Steamship fleet. One morning we visited the wharf and joined a mixed group of Hindoos, Chinese, Japanese and Whites assembled there to bid adieu to friends or relatives on their way to the Orient, Australia or the far North, Alaska or Yukon, or the South. Three large steamers were leaving about the same time, and yet there was little excitment among the passengers, or those left behind. It was a contrast to the departure of an Atlantic liner from Quebec or New York.

We approached a handsome looking Hindoo with a large turban on his head, and asked if he was returning home, to which he replied :

" Yes."

" How long have you been here ? "

" Three years."

" As you going to return to Canada ? "

" No, me find work too hard. India not so much mountains ; not so much cold ; me make enough money to buy land and work at home."

We noticed he stood beside the gangway, leading to the fore part of the ship, while the Chinese seemed to be lodged in the aft, so we asked him whether he did not associate with the Celestials.

" Hindoo and Mohammedans, no like Chinamen or Japanese, only go with white man. "

Almost all the Hindous we have seen, and there are quite a number in the western towns, retain the turban portion of their dress, though wearing the remainder of the European costume, They are a good looking lot, but slothful as compared with Canadians. The Japanese seem to be very unpopular,

168

1. Sailing Vessels in Port Vancouver, B.C.
2. Esquimault Dry Dock.
3. C. P. R. Empress Hotel, Vancouver, B.C.

and the Chinese are given the preference on every occasion of choice. This was ludicrously explained to us by a Vancouver policeman, of whom we had asked why the Japanese were held in such disparagement by the western people. He said :

" Well, I will explain the difference. If a Chinaman says he is going to kill you, you can bank on him doing it some day whether it takes him a life time to carry out his threat, but with a Japanese, you never know whether he will or will not; he is treacherous, cowardly and untruthful alongside of the Chinese, who is exceptionally honest and reliable in all his transactions."

We never should have thought so, nor do we think that the lordly officer had arrived at the proper conclusion, but we presume that the element of Japanese, which is coming to America, is in a very great measure similar to some of our English immigrants, who have been classed under the heading of " Undesirables." To all outward appearance the Japanese do not give one any such evidence of their unfavorable character.

The salmon catches and canneries are one of the interesting features of Vancouver.

The salmon come up the river in shoals of hundreds of thousands, judging by the stories one hears. On the Fraser, and other rivers, in such large numbers that they not only raise the waters, but crowd themselves out of the rivers upon the banks, where they rot in thousands unless carted away by the farmers of the district, to be used as a fertilizer upon the soil. There are ever so many immense canneries, giving employment to thousands of laborers, while the plants are going night and day during the time the runs are on. These inrushes of salmon are of different varieties and go up the rivers at different periods of the year, first having to run the gauntlet of the American fishermen's nets before making their way into Canadian waters. During our visit a peculiar incident, in connection with this industry, was illustrated.

We found the Vancouverites bitterly complaining of the poor run of Sockeye salmon, and they came to the conclusion that the Americans had made too big a net haul, leaving a very small number to reach the Canadian waters, but, to the surprise of every one, the run commenced a few days after the expected time or season, which is immediately after they have arrived in the American waters, and all the best informed salmon experts were at a loss for an explanation for the strange conduct of this particular variety of salmon. The following newspaper extract, taken from one of the local papers during our visit, gives an explanation of the deep Pacific, which extract appeared in a

170

1. Salmon Fleet, Vancouver.
2. Bringing in Salmon.
3. Part of a Salmon Catch.

Seattle daily paper, during our stay in that city :

" The recent experiences of the canneries on the Fraser river show how little is really known about the habits of the salmon, and how seriously those who have made the closest study of them may be mistaken. On the American side of the line the run of sockeye salmon a few weeks ago was the greatest ever known and the canneries were working their forces to the point of utter exhaustion in order to take care of the great catches made. The salmon were merely passing through American waters on their way to their spawning grounds on the Fraser.

" Singularly enough, the great salmon run failed fully to materialize in the Fraser, and the catch there was disappointingly small, as compared with that on the American side of the line. The run was over some weeks since, with a lamentably poor showing, and there was a tendency to claim that so many fish had been taken on the American side of the line that there were none left for the fishermen in British Columbia waters.

" Now, some weeks after the run of these salmon was supposed to be over and long after the fish had disappeared from American waters on this side of the boundary line, the largest run of sockeye of the season has appeared in the mouth of the Fraser River. Millions of them are appearing, the

171

fishermen are making great catches, and the cannery men have every prospect of being able to fill the hundreds of thousands of empty tins left on their hands when the summer run of fish ceased. The fish are also reported to be in prime condition. "

There is always a late run of sockeyes, but there are some surface indications to warrant the belief that the present great run includes fish which passed American waters some weeks since, but which, for some reason, did not enter the Fraser at that time.

To give an idea of the importance of Salmon Packing industry to British Columbia, it may be mentioned that the fisheries of this province have yielded one hundred and thirteen million dollars. Last year halibut establishments from Vancouver alone totalled 19,472,000 lbs., and were valued at $933,600.

1. Drawing the Salmon Seines near Vancouver.
2. Unloading the Salmon.
3. 60,000 Cans of Salmon.

CHAPTER XX

Vancouver to Victoria

THE GROWTH of Vancouver is phenomenal; in 1887, the population was three thousand and now it is close on to one hundred thousand, while the growth of the value of assessable property during the last ten years, is shown in the following table :

1899.	$17,716,289 00
1900.	19,553,645 00
1901.	20,233,130 00
1902.	21,065,370 00
1903.	22,936,835 00
1904.	24,688,855 00
1905.	28,543,890 00
1906.	39,189,400 00
1907.	54,727,810 00
1908.	61,854,850 00

1909—Unrevised assessment shows an increase of 10 millions or a total of $71,-000,000.00.

This is more than three times the assessment valuation of Quebec, with a population of over 75,000 inhabitants.

Vancouver is also contiguous to an excellent dairy country, principally along the Fraser River, where the farmers are said to grow twice as much food per acre as is usually grown on other farm lands.   Mr. F. M. Logan, of the Hygienic Dairy, is authority for the statement that there are some farms, which produce five tons of hay, two thousand bushels of roots, and one hundred bushels of grain per acre, and the grazing is equally as good.

The climate is mild in winter, and cool in summer, the rains of the former season are about the only objectionable feature, and this the people get used to.

The lumber and mining assets of British Columbia, of which Vancouver will richly reap the benefit, are immense, and but slightly developed so far. The cut of lumber in 1907 was valued at $12,680.000. The coal mines are estimated to be capable of an output of ten million tons of coal per annum, for seven thousand years, while the gold mines have thus far yielded $114,000.00.00.

Orchards in British Columbia in 1901 covered 7,880 acres, and in 1908, 100,000 acres, while the fruit shipments, such as apples, peaches, pears, plums and grapes in 1902, amounted to 1,956 tons and in 1908 6,243 tons, and last year probably doubled this quantity.

And yet British Columbia to-day has still on hand some ten million acres of wheat lands, and four million acres of fruit lands, for the future newcomers.

What we like about this western country is the fact that everybody who lives there

174

1. Vancouver from Mt. Pleasant.
2. Lake Louise, from a painting.

is a booster for his city, or district, and their boosting is backed up with such evident facts that there is no doubting them. It is our belief, that the most sanguine forecasts, are none too exaggerated, to be realized some day. It is simply, a matter of time. There will be many setbacks and many obstacles to be surmounted before the great dream of every Westerner is realized, but the fight will eventually be won, for never was a population of human beings so steeled in ardor of determination, optimism and courage, than you will meet in Canada's Great West.

We left Vancouver, not with regret, for we were to return there again on our homeward journey. We travelled on one of the Canadian Pacific Railway steamships, running between Vancouver, Victoria and Seattle. The distance to Victoria is eighty miles and the voyage is full of picturesqueness, while the steamships and service are beyond all expectations of the Easterner. We have nothing in the East to compare with them.

Those who have travelled on these boats will know what we mean ; those who have not may take our word for it until they do. There is not a better organization of polite officers and stewards to be found anywhere.

And you marvel at it all when you make the voyage. The several steamships employed in this service are models of comfort. Long may they maintain this record, for it is gratifying to be told this by every American we meet, and the majority of passengers on board are Americans. We should not overlook making mention of the meals which were in keeping with everything else on board and could not be surpassed by the leading hotels on land.

Victoria was reached in five hours, and we wended our way through a sinuous channel of islands into its harbor where we caught sight of the copper roof of the Empress Hotel, another of the Canadian Pacific Railway hotels, then the hotel itself, in its solitary grandeur, a few hundred feet away from where we docked. It stands in a large open space in the centre of the town, with the beautiful Parliament Buildings on the right, and the new Post Office on the left. If the site of the hotel appears to the visitor as seeming lonely, he must remember that this will disappear in time, when it is surrounded by a growth of tropical trees, gardens of roses and other beautiful floral blooms. We are prompted to make these statements, for one of the greatest surprises which awaits the newly arrived on entering the house is the air of refinement and sumptuousness that almost takes away your breath. Before you register your name you realize that you have fallen in love with the hotel. It appeals

1. C. P. R. Empress Hotel, Victoria, B.C.
2. Palm Room, Empress Hotel.
3. C. P. R. Steamer Princess Victoria.

to you in the dining room, in the palm room, with its cozy looking green tables and chairs to match and everything tempting to enjoy the tranquil scene, so refreshing to the travel-ler, but, surprises do not end here. Parlors and bedrooms are equally charming, and we cannot refrain from saying that for those suffering from nervous troubles we advise them to go to the Empress Hotel at Victoria, and if they do not find an immediate cure, then their case is hopeless. The manager, Mr. Humble, and the waiters and bell-boys, made us feel as though we were an honored guest in a castle, rather than an ordinary guest in a hotel but when we interviewed the manager, for we could not leave without complimenting him upon the excellent service, he said :—" Well, we try to make everyone feel that this is a home, and not a hotel." In our experience there are few hotel men who accomplish this, but from all we heard and saw, in and around the Empress at Victoria, we must admit that our host comes nearer to it than any other we have known.

Victoria is not a large city, nor does it boast of any of the Western boosting pro-pensities of the inhabitants of the mainland. It is ordinary and more set in its ways. Those who live in Victoria enjoy life without many thoughts of the future. Mainland men come over and start up real estate offices, and endeavor to stir up its inhabitants, but it is of no use. Victoria was born before any of the main coast or interior western cities, and it does not want to brag so much of its coal fields and other natural assets, because it knows that their development will come in due course. In the meantime, a large number of its citizens believe in the theory that they will be a long time dead and there is no use of hurrying to the end.

We drove around Victoria for three hours and saw the most of it. There were some fine stores and residences, but no life, that is to say, none of the bustling activity seen in the West from the time we arrived in Port Arthur. Even the stores we entered displayed a lethargic state of reposeful service and attendance, and in one, perhaps better known than any other store in Victoria, where celebrated sweetmeats were sold, we were told that frequently it was closed at noon, or, whenever the stock was sold out. This store occupies one of the most central business sites in the city. Independence is no name for the character of the proprietor of this business, and we thought ourselves fortunate to find the establishment open, thus offering us an opportunity of purchasing several pounds of bonbons, the most delicious sweets we have ever tasted, and only costing 75 cts. per pound. The best New York bonbons at $2.00 per pound, could not hold a patch on them.

In driving around the city, between the hours of five and seven o'clock, in the evening, we were surprised to notice that there were very few people out of doors. Our cabby informed us that the Victorians seldom left their houses during these hours as, they were "eating hours," wherein, we judged the Victoria people to be a very conservative population. We saw the Governor's residence and grounds, which latter should have shown more beautiful lawns and floral embellishments than they did. In fact, we were greatly disappointed in Victoria in this respect, as we had gone there with such great expectations. Most of the houses in the residential parts are entirely hidden from view by stone and wooden fences—or green hedges very much similar to what one sees in Great Britain. The buildings are also characteristic of Old England, and the occupants are better found through the names of their houses on the gate posts than through the number in the streets. Victoria was an old Hudson Bay post before the railway stretched across Western Canada, and was used by this company, as a fur trading and store-house on the Pacific coast.

Hunting, fishing, and duck shooting are very excellent on Vancouver Island, and during the short stay of twenty-four hours, we had the opportunity of catching, before breakfast, two fine salmon, weighing $5\frac{1}{2}$ and

7 lbs. respectively. There is very little difficulty in such a sporting achievement if you
happen to be in the city during the run of
salmon, as was our good fortune. You
simply leave an order at the hotel office to be
called at 5 a.m., and at 5.30 o'clock, you are
comfortably seated in a launch, heading for
the outer bay, which you reach in a few
minutes. Then you let out your trolling
line, with no bait on the end of it, only a
tin troll, and then keep gasolining about
for an hour or two. You invariably meet
with success, sometimes catching as many
as twenty-five or thirty salmon. We must
say that the British Columbia salmon is not
as palatable as that caught in our Saguenay
River, nor is it so tender.

We visited Esquimault, which in the West
is not pronounced as it is in Quebec, but is
given an entirely English accent. Here we
found little visible signs of life. The officer
at the gate said we could not enter without
an order, as all the men were away and that
there was nothing doing at the time as the
Canadian Government were talking of taking
over the fort and ship-yard, and he wished
they would do so pretty quickly as it was a
shame to see such a fine place in such absolute
idleness.

We inspected the dry dock, which was
very dry and empty at the time, but it seemed
to suffer from the same trouble as the St.

Joseph dock, at Quebec. It is altogether too small for present day requirements.

Harold Sands, a well-known writer in "Collier's," recently said :—"Two years ago a Toronto judge visited Vancouver. At Westminster Junction, a few miles from the city, a deputation was on the platform waiting to welcome him 'to our midst.' The judge thought the well dressed distinguished looking men, who sought him in the parlor car, were brother jurists, or at least the Mayor and part of the corporation. To his dismay, the strangers introduced themselves as real estate men, who had 'the finest proposition, Judge, to double your money in a year.' The Toronto man couldn't resist their blandishments and he invested. If he hasn't sold out at a good profit it is only because he is looking for a larger wad, for Vancouver property is in the airship class now—it is so high up. Before returning East the Judge went across the Gulf of Georgia to Victoria. He tells the rest of his story thus : 'There was nobody in sight. I went into a store to buy something. There was no one to wait on me. Finally I leaned over the counter, spied a clerk, held him up by the collar, and forced him to make me a sale.'

"Cities of marked characteristics, like forcible persons, always get nicknames. Every Canadian knows what envious Hamilton calls Toronto or Halifax calls St. John, or Toronto calls Montreal. Equally familiar is the reason why Irving referred to New Yorkers as Gothamites. On the Pacific coast the somewhat jealous people of Victoria and New Westminster speak of Vancouver as the City of Greed. They assert and their " langwidge," as Sam Weller used to say, is beautiful—that it " wants to hog everything." Vancouver gracefully retaliates by referring to the town on the Fraser as the Royal City, because Queen Victoria christened it, and cheerfully styles Victoria a pleasant place to go to sleep in.

" Parliament Buildings, dead things themselves, cannot give life to a city. Victoria is a calm and peaceful place. In this lovely spot where the can't-be-hurried people gather roses at Christmas, not even ten changes of ministries, in twenty years, caused one real ripple of excitement.

" Perhaps the chief reason why Victoria has been so quickly outrun by Vancouver, is that while the latter was established by Canadians and Americans, the former is essentially an English city. Founded by men sent out from the old country by the Hudson Bay Company, it still retains some of the characteristics of the Victorian era which have been discarded in the home land, and so its people are now spoken of as more English than the English. They were immensely tickled when a wandering

London journalist spoke of Victoria as the 'finest colonial copy of Mayfair within the bounds of the Empire,' and they will always maintain on their visiting lists the writer who spoke of them as 'a colony of British gentlefolk.' "

Signs are not wanting, however, that Victoria, is beginning to awaken from its long sleep. Real estate men from Vancouver and Winnipeg observe that men who have made fortunes in the wheat fields are gravitating there to dwell in comparative ease. But the leisure of a prairie man is vastly different from that of the practised Englishman. The man who has lived a busy life is active even when at rest, and the new blood at the capital is bringing about a change. The retired naval, military, and Hudson Bay officers are gradually dying off and a more vigorous stock is taking their places.

Street Scene at Seattle during the Great Fair.

CHAPTER XXI

Seattle and the Great Exhibition—Return to Vancouver

WE PAID a visit to Seattle and the Alaskan. Yukon Pacific Exhibition, which was an unqualified success, as the final financial reports have demonstrated. The show was not as large as that of St. Louis or Chicago, but it was most unique in its site and architecture. The Exhibition covered two hundred and fifty acres and cost ten millions of dollars, while the exhibits were valued at fifty millions. The cascade in the vicinity of the Arctic circle, over which flowed fourteen thousand gallons of water per minute was a marvelous sight and held the thousands of spectators, who assembled within the grounds, in mute amazement. The floral display about the grounds and the forestry building were, to our mind, the features of the exhibition. The former covered many acres and made a veritable bower of all descriptions of flowers in full bloom.

The history of Seattle is as wonderful as that of Vancouver or any of the Canadian Western towns which we have mentioned. Some years ago it was in a stagnant condition, so depressed and low spirited, that its merchants were on the eve of general bankruptcy, to which may possibly be ascribed the reason for their getting together and making a strenuous effort to discover the reasons for the stagnation and to hit upon a solution for improving the business of the future. At a public meeting called for the purpose of discussing this subject the question of advertising the city was brought up and strongly supported by the leading business men, who subscribed a large amount of money to make the city known throughout the United States and all the countries of the world. It was not long before the effects of this advertising was felt, and with renewed energy and vigor, and with brighter hopes, the merchants began to see signs of better days and a general air of optimism prevailed, and with it came the gold discoveries of the Yukon, which they took advantage of by sending travellers to the North, and being the first salesmen on the ground, they sold millions of dollars of goods, and soon got control of the trade of the Yukon. This was the turning point of Seattle. Since then it has been going ahead at such a rapid rate that it has a population to-day close on to three hundred thousand.

The city controls its water system and electric light plant. It covers seventy-eight square miles, fifty inland and twenty-eight in water. It has a fine harbor with a large fleet of steamers carrying freight and passengers to all points on the Pacific Coast, as well as to the Orient. The commerce for this port for the year 1908, amounted to over one hundred and twenty-four millions of dollars.

During our visit we were very much interested in the Public Civic Works, which were under way and to cost many millions of dollars. The object of these improvements was to level the city which is built, like Rome, upon a number of hills. The city is now expending vast sums in lowering and raising streets. The cost of which, though restricted to one district, is borne by the whole population. Seattle is strict in its observance of the license law. It is impossible to obtain a drink of any intoxicating liquor on Sunday, nor is it permissible to serve such drinks, with meals, in the public hotels, or even in the rooms of the guests. Under no circumstances will the hotel management dare take the risk of breaking this steadfast rule.

We left Seattle at night, and arrived in Vancouver the next morning.

The Sockeye salmon were running when we returned to the capital city. We were fortunate in seeing the Stevenson cannery in full operation, night and day, for the salmon have to be caught and canned during the week or so that they are on the run. The work was most interesting and one of the sights of the west coast. We stood on a pier and saw thousands upon thousands of salmon, piled up in huge pyramids like coal heaps. They were being received from small yawls, outfitted with gasoline engines, and principally manned by Japanese, who gathered up the salmon at stated periods from the smaller boats, fishing about a mile or two from the shore. Here hung out a formidable gauntlet of fishing lines and nets, almost across the mouth of the Fraser River through which the Sockeye were endeavoring to make their way in order to deposit their spawn, many miles up the flowing stream, or, as far as they could go, and then, die by the thousands through being crowded upon the shores of either side of the river. Here they are left to rot, unless carried away by the local farmers, to be used as a fertilizer for the nearby lands.

From the big heaps of salmon all beautifully fresh and weighing from five to fifteen pounds, making an average of about seven pounds, the larger salmon being the exception to the rule, they are hooked and placed upon a table where their heads and tails are rapidly removed, then they are placed through a machine that rips them up and cleans out their insides in the twinking of an eye. After this treatment they are passed to a lot of Hindoos, Japanese and Indians, men and women, who give them a few

1. The Three Sisters, from a painting.
2. Old Cariboo Road Bridge, Fraser River Canon.

finishing touches, trim their fins, after which
they are chopped into small pieces by hand
and jammed into tin boxes, sealed up and
placed in large steam ovens to be boiled
into the state in which they are found when
they reach the dining tables of the Easterners,
although a very large quantity of the salmon
is shipped to England and other European
ports, in vessels which make the trip around
Cape Horn. While on this subject there is
no doubt in the most of minds that the opening of the Panama Canal will do much to add
to Vancouver's prosperity, for it will probably make a new and cheaper channel for
western grain accommodation and for con-
veying goods to Western Canada.

Vancouver should be a great tourist centre,
it is contiguous to so many beautiful ocean
trips, such as the Yukon, Prince Rupert
Land, Victoria, Seattle, etc. The prime factor
of its enterprise and go aheadness is to
be found in its real live business men, who
are working in the interest of Vancouver.
Then there is its Tourist Association, which
has done a wonderful work, but unlike the
Quebec organization, they are seen and heard
of constantly, spreading literature and giving
information to the thousands of people who
are seeking it.

A number of Quebecers are doing business
in Vancouver among whom are Messrs.
Borden, H. G. Ross, and Beau Gowan,

all of whom are in real estate and doing exceedingly well.

We were sorry to leave Vancouver, for it had made such a good impression upon us that we would have liked to have extended our visit a few days, to see more of it and more of its people. It is not crowded— not so crowded as Winnipeg or Seattle. There are so many points in its favor that one cannot help having a great respect for what it is and what its future is likely to be We have no hesitation in saying that of all the Western cities, none show such unmistakable signs of rapid and continuous growth, as Vancouver. Real estate has increased some 33 per cent, during the past year, and while many visitors claim the prices have soared too high, the knowing ones are still " plunging " and making money, and even if a re-action were to set in, it would only be temporary for the foundation of this city is well laid.

While Vancouver is practically without manufacturing, it is largely benefited by the prairie farmer, who, having achieved success and fortune, retires to the coast to spend the remainder of his days amid congenial surroundings and in a less rigorous climate.

We did not remain in Vancouver long enough to pry into its civic administration, but from the little we saw, or, the little we did not see, we think its municipal council could put on a spurt in the making of roads and necessary improvements, in the new parts of the town, which, in comparison with what is being done in Edmonton, Winnipeg and Seattle, certainly displays a want of progressive public spirit in this direction. It may be said that this is due to a scarcity of labor, or, the too rapid growth of the city, but, even then, it seems to us that they are poor excuses to put forth, if we were in any way right in our conjecture. But all these things right themselves in time, and as we said before, we more than regretted our departure, and as we said au revoir to kind friends who saw us off at the station, we meant it, for we intend to return again to see the realization of our forecast of this far-off Western city.

As we began our homeward journey, we could not dispel the impressions of our trip West, but it was not altogether at an end, for we had yet to see the Arrow Head and Kootenay lakes, via the Crow's Nest Pass route, which branches off from the Canadian Pacific Railway main line at Revelstoke and takes a south-easterly direction. We soon realized that there was little, in the way of scenery, which could surpass that which we had seen in the Rockies and Selkirks, but we were yet to see the great mining district of the West! We were to pass by coal, lead and silver mines, the output of which was

191

tending to still further enrich the wealth
of this great Dominion. Our journey had
not occupied, as yet, a month, and we
had sufficient days to reach home before
that time had elapsed, and yet, we considered
we had seen what every good Canadian
should see. Therefore, it is " up to " those
who may read these notes of this Western
journey to take up the trail for themselves,
and do as we have done. Canada will be
better off for having her sons and daughters
educated to the magnitude and richness of
their Dominion. It has been given to us,
and no one will deny that the Westerners
are not making the best of it, but it is so
broad and so deep, that it will take many
hundreds of thousands to join the trail
with pack and train to help open up the
unknown and silent places ; to bring forth
the minerals, which lie in hiding.

Nature has provided them with coal and
timber, as well as lakes and rivers teeming
with fish, to allay any fears of starvation or of
suffering from the varying changes of climatic
conditions.

In the West you will find men who think ;
men who are brave, courteous and chival-
rous ; men who protect the women and the
young ; men who are kind and generous ;
men who uphold the right and condemn the
wrong ; men who boast, but do not brag ;
men who talk common sense and hate the

192

liar and pessimist. What more does a country require to make it a great nation of broad-minded men and women ?

We met numbers of Americans and all had a good word for the West. Few were wont to brag about their own lands to the south of us. They seemed to join hands with their Canadian neighbors and give them the encouragement which they themselves cherished when opening up their own country. There was the ring of real true, genuine friend-ship, in their exclamations of appreciation of the various new settlements which we passed, whether from train, or from steamer.

They were better judges of the grain, vegetable and fruit growing possibilities of the country, than we were, and it had the effect of convincing us that such universal testimony, coming from strangers of a neigh-boring republic, on a visit, like ourselves, in Western Canada, to see and learn, was the strongest kind of evidence as to the wonderful richness of this land.

While travelling on the boat from Victoria to Seattle we noticed a large number of American farmers returning from a visit to Canada, and invariably their conversation drifted to the fine lands they had seen from the car windows.

" Say," said one farmer to another, " did you see that country coming up here ? "

" Yes," replied his newly-made acquaintance.

" Well, isn't it good, say ! I am going to
come up again and look it over. It seems
to me I ought to have some of that," and
this is about the way most of the American
farmers think on their way home, after
looking the country over.

1. Crow's Nest Mountain.
2. Sentinel Valley, near Crow's Nest.

CHAPTER XXII

Vancouver to Crow's Nest Pass

IT WAS late in the afternoon of the day of our departure from Vancouver, when we left the main line of the Canadian Pacific Railway for our southern trip through the Crow's Nest Pass, which was to bring us through considerable waterways until we again reached the main line at Medicine Hat.

The next morning, at Arrowhead, we embarked on a light draft paddle wheel steamer for West Robson, a delightful sail over a beautiful sheet of water, hemmed in by mountain slopes, not so high as the Rockies, but, nevertheless, quite picturesque. Along the route we passed small settlements of homesteaders principally engaged in fruit culture, a fine hotel at a sulphur spring where good hunting and fishing is obtained, and a few mines, until at nightfall we reached our destination, where, we found a train in readiness to convey us over fifty mile of track to Nelson. Here we had the opportunity of making a tour of this enterprising town which was all in fête attire and brilliantly illuminated with strings of electric lamps, in honor of a fruit fair, which had opened that day.

In Nelson we found a fine broad main

street with excellent up-to-date stores, some of them large and modern enough to make us think that we were in a city of ten times the population ; it is only about eight thousand in all. Several large buildings including a branch bank, the Post-Office, and several school houses embellished the city. That night we slept on board the steamer " Kaskanook," and at six the next morning we were steaming up the Kootenay Lake, arriving at Kootenay Landing about ten o'clock. Here we boarded a train and started out on our tour through what is known as the Crow's Nest proper. It is the big coal, lead and silver mining district of British Columbia and the North West.

Shortly after leaving the landing we witnessed the extraordinary sight of several thousand geese (waivies) and ducks along the borders of the Kootenay River and in Duck lake. We considered this one of the most interesting game spectacles we had seen on the whole of our trip West, outside of the salmon catches on the Fraser River. Further West we passed the cities of Fernie,Cranbrook, Hosmer, Michel, Frank, Hillcrest, Macleod, Lethbridge, and the next morning, Medicine Hat, where we returned to the main line of the Canadian Pacific Railway and train No. 96, well known to the western travellers, as are Nos. 6, 95 and 5. Many of the foregoing places are mining towns, with hundreds

of coke ovens blazing away, which in the
night time threw a lurid glare upon the
mountain slopes and lit up the valleys with
brilliant reflections.

Fernie is in the centre of the largest coal
area in America and has over seven hundred
coke ovens. On Moyle Lake there are very
large deposits of silver and lead ore, while
Macleod and Old Man River are the most
typical of western ranching towns where the
"Horse is still King." It is the headquarters of the ranching district of southern
Alberta. By this short description the reader
may judge of the interest attaching to a
visit, either going West, or returning East,
via the Crow's Nest Pass, for during our two
days and two nights, and notwithstanding
the fact that we were travelling almost
continuously through a·mountainous country,
we passed most thriving and prosperous
looking towns, and along no part of the
Canadian Pacific Railway was there more
diversified interests, such as mineral, lumbering and agriculture.

We might mention that the Arrowlake
district, which promises to be another fruit-
growing area similar to the Okanagan Valley,
is but little under cultivation and is worth
an inspection by those, whose means are
limited, whereas those with money, would
do better to enter the Okanagan Valley.

The boats on the Crow's Nest Pass waterways are under the control of the Canadian Pacific Railway system which also runs car scows as well to convey train loads of freight cars from one end to the other. The service on the boats is equal to that of any inland navigation company—the boats of the fleet having spacious dining and parlor saloons, with all modern conveniences, and an excellent cuisine. The service is daily, excepting Sundays, running both ways, and is carried on throughout the entire year, the weather not being cold enough in winter to freeze the lakes—in fact, the mercury seldom registers below freezing point. The steamers stop here and there to take on, or let off passengers by simply running half-steam ashore, the beaches on either side of the lake being sandy so there is no danger of doing any damage to the boats.

While travelling through the Kootenay Lakes a pathetic incident was brought to our notice. We met an aged couple from Jamestown, Pa. The old man, seemed fatigued and remarked to his devoted little wife, that he wished they had reached their destination for he was very tired, and he wondered " if James would be there to meet them." We were drawn into conversation with the old lady, who told us the sad story of their lives. Many years ago their only son had left them for the Canadian North West. They had never heard from him again not-

198

1. Medicine Hat
2. Elevator, Indian Head.
3. Moose Jaw Hotel and Station.

withstanding they had done everything to locate him. The thought of the absent boy, as years fled on, and the chances that they might probably never meet him again, weighed so heavily upon the old man that his brain had become slightly affected. His only comfort was travelling through the West, looking into every corner, and making enquiries for his missing boy. This aged couple had spent the summer visiting almost all the small villages and towns in the West, and were returning by the Crow's Nest Pass, still looking for their James.

From the railway station at Medicine Hat we obtained an excellent view of the surrounding country, which showed to advantage under a blue sky and bright sunshine, the same sunshine which we have spoken of so often and which seemed to follow us throughout our entire trip. We had returned again to the prairie land, that land of tall grass, and cattle ranches, and as we journeyed on for a hundred miles we looked out of the car windows. In all directions, North and South we saw numerous large herds of cattle and horses, with here and there a coyote who showed no fear at our approach, but on the contrary stood in curious pose and gazed upon the long string of Pullman and parlor cars go by. We also passed large flocks of geese in and around small lakes. Close by the line we saw hundreds of railway labourers burning the grass between the track and the furrows, to prevent prairie fires from spreading North or South. It was a land of fat cattle and prosperity, and we listened to the exultant exclamations of our fellow passengers upon the millions of acres of land to be seen everywhere awaiting the newcomers. Then we passed into the wheat areas of Southern Alberta, and Saskatchewan, and the crops were not all cut or harvested by any means. This fact gave us an opportunity of seeing the threshing of grain and the piling up of thousands of huge stacks of straw, which are afterwards burned. The day previous, and on many other days, we had been looking upon millions of feet of timber going to waste, through fire and old age, or being burned up by the mills, and now we were viewing a wanton waste of straw and grasses. Some day all this waste will be of value, for man will yet find use for it, but to-day its loss is one of the amazing sights of the West. It must no doubt astonish our English fellow travellers more than it does the Eastern Canadian, but this is not the only waste of the prairie, as thousands of tons of flax are allowed to rot in the ground for want of labor to cut it, and because there are no mills to use it, and the reason there are no mills is because the labor to run them would be too expensive to make them pay. Only the seed is gathered which commands a good market value. We passd Moose Jaw and Regina, two good-looking towns, the former having 14,000 and the latter nearly the same population. We also, passed Swift Current and Brandon, the latter having 15,000, and Portage la Prairie, with 10,000 inhabitants, and in every one of these towns the motor car seemed to be the predominant means of locomotion.

We also passed a freight train with four threshing machines, and were told that almost every freight train going west was carrying thousands of dollars worth of the very latest agricultural machinery, and that it was nothing to what came out before the harvesting season began. Furthermore, that the farming machinery thus going out was only for use next year.

At Moose Jaw we met an old Quebecer, Mr. Jack Vicque, who is manager of the Union Bank of that city. He is about as optimistic a banking man as resides in the West. He told us of several of his customers who were ranchers, and who would each clear over $20,000 with the season's crop, and as most of them were out of debt this money was a clean surplus over and above their unencumbered ranch, and many thousands of dollars worth of machinery.

Mr. Vicque was so enthusiastic about the growth of Moose Jaw, and was so solicitous about our seeing Winnipeg and the other cities, that it put us in mind of a story told us while in the West by a well known English newspaper man, who had used it in his des-cription of the rapid growth of the towns and the optimism of their people. It is the story of the man from Winnipeg.

" Seen Winnipeg ? " he said to the Toronto man. " Why yes," replied the latter, " I was there a week ago." " Ah, but you should see Winnipeg now."

Then our English journalist friend conti-nues his story of the wonderful develop-ment of the West as follows :

" —' Semper mutabile '—such is the charm of the Fair Dominion. To-day we see the last car of a freight train carrying a ready-made station to be dropped down somewhere on the line on desolate prairie. To-morrow finds a tented village. On the next day a hotel, a store, an elevator, a livery stable and a Bon Ton millinery parlor. Within a week the Board of Trade has issued an adver-tising pamphlet entitled: ' We are it.' ' Watch us grow.' If such a growth can happen in a week, think of the progress of two years.

" Sometimes this summer, as I rambled through a Western Canadian city, I could have fancied myself in a vast builder's yard. An army of men at work in the streets. Another army swarmed upon the half finished houses, and upon the frames of steel and concrete shooting up on corner lots."

" The prairie told the self same tale. Tents and shacks, ready-made and half-made houses lined the railroad track from Bassano west to Calgary, where, memory recalled, two years ago, a rancher's country untenanted except by scattered droves of cattle.

" Was Strathmore there when I last passed through ? I don't remember. But this time Strathmore thrust itself upon me with a main street full of rigs and livery stables and busy stores.

" An elevator, three weeks old, land-marked the station. Another elevator, two weeks old was under way, while the timber for the third filled the freight train on the siding.

" Was Langdon in existence when I last passed through ? I cannot recollect. Langdon now says that Strathmore is a back number, while the neighboring Gleichen, another of those sudden cities, claims to have outpaced them all.

"The man who drawns the map of West Canada must have a breathless time."

CHAPTER XXIII

Regina to Winnipeg

ABOUT DUSK that evening we stopped at Regina for ten minutes and took advantage of it for a walk on the platform for a breath of fresh air, although we could not complain of either dust or coal soot during our lengthy travel across the continent.

This is another advantage of the Canadian Pacific route over the American lines.

As we walked up and down the board station walk we asked our porter what kind of a city Regina was.

" Well," he replied, " I guess it's a pretty good town, because the chief of police and the Governor dine together and I guess that's good enough for anyone."

His answer was meant to convey the idea that aristocracy, in the home of the Government in this new Western province, had not as yet made any class distinction.

" Porter," we continued, " why don't you settle in this Western province ? "

" Well, sir," he responded, " that is what I intend to do pretty soon. I've got a homestead of 160 acres in Edmonton, and as soon as I get it in order I intend to give up railroading ".

And this was not the first railroad employee

we had met and questioned on the same subject, and nearly everyone of them had some land interest, either in city real estate, homesteads, or fruitlands.

One of the waiters on one of the boats plying on the Kootenay lakes, had sixteen acres of land in the Okanagan Valley, for which he had paid $2,500, and this was his last season to serve on table. Although he could have turned over his investment at a nice profit he preferred to keep it and make it his future home.

This is the spirit all through the West, among almost every class of railway employees, or, officials,—in fact, it is in evidence everywhere. The people have faith in the future of the West, and their faith is not without reason. This is why, in a great measure, the Canadian Pacific Railway, and other big railway corporations, are credited with such excellent servants. They all have a self interest in the upbuilding of the country.

In Winnipeg, we know of a hotel chef who arrived there a little over a year ago, with $3,000. and for some reason or other, bought land along the river front at Saint-Boniface. Six months afterwards, he showed his bank account to the manager of his hotel; it showed a deposit of $25,000. The Canadian Northern wanted the land and bought it at a big advance. The chef afterwards invested the money in other properties and to-day he is worth $50,000. He has now no desire to return East, or even to give up his position as chef of one of the leading Western hotels. We could go on giving examples of like cases, but what is the use. They might cause the less experienced to invest unwisely, and perhaps lose all they have through the sharks in the real estate business, and for this we would have to assume some responsibility. We prefer to advise those who have money to invest to first visit the West—then judge for themselves.

The next morning we were in Winnipeg, the approach to which afforded us the same endless visions of immense areas of golden fields, similar to those we had passed the day before, and no doubt during the night, for we had travelled through the district surrounding Brandon, the centre of Manitoba's most fertile wheat area, where sixty bushels to an acre was a common record this year.

A brilliant sun shone from a cloudless sky, the same azure sky that had been our constant canopy during our whole month.

We took advantage of our one day's stay in the capital of Manitoba to call upon Mr. Bruce Walker, the Canadian Commissioner of Immigration, in the handsome Dominion Government buildings, adjoining the Canadian Pacific Railway hotel and station.

We wanted to know something about the vast crop of wheat, and we could obtain more authentic information from him than from any one else in Canada. We were not wrong in this assumption, for we found Mr. Walker. not only a painstaking Government official, but a man with such a sense of responsibility, that one would think that he had the whole of Central Canada, or, the wants of that great country, under his special care, and from all we saw and heard, he certainly is leaving no stone unturned in fittingly and faithfully doing his duty towards supplying the farmers with what they require. This was not accomplished without a considerable amount of worrying, this season, for in his own words, " it was nothing but an act of Providence in providing a continuous spell of sunshine for six consecutive weeks, which fact alone was responsible for the great fall harvest, for had the weather been unfavorable, certainly one quarter of the crop would have been destroyed for the lack of labor to gather it in."

There was a happy radiance and irresistible good humor about Mr. Walker on the morning we met him, and when we told him our mission, he was quick in getting down to facts, and stating exactly what the people of the West wanted the people of the East to know, and how the latter could assist the former.

" You know," said Mr. Walker, in his fine Scotch accent, " the labor question is the great problem with the wheat grower, and has to be solved in a manner of mutual interest between both ends of this great Dominion. We have had a narrow escape this year, but I have a suggestion which I hope to see carried out, which will give the West a permanent supply of seven thousand harvesters every year, and which I wish you would take up and assist me in making public. You know the agricultural implement manufacturers are in the habit of closing down their establishments for a month or so, commencing from the middle of September. Now, if we can get them to do this about the middle of August instead we will have several thousands of employees, who will be glad of the opportunity of making some money during this idle holiday, and at the same time assisting the West, and in doing this they would be assisting the largest consumers of agricultural implements, for let it be known that 65 per cent of the agricultural implements manufactured in Canada are sold in the West, leaving 35 per cent for the remainder of the Dominion and for export."

" There is, however, a possible objection to this. The manufacturers may think that their men would not return to the East again. This would be a mistaken idea for these men as a rule are steady, reliable workers, and after the crop was harvested there would be no further work for them, so it would not be in their interest to remain in the West. Again, their families and all their interests would be still in the East, and in all probability, or, with few exceptions, they would return to their respective factories, and the small percentage of those who would remain, would be only those who contemplated going out in any event. Even then it would only mean an additional purchase of rakes, ploughs, binders and other machinery, so that it would not be an unmixed evil or loss to the manufacturer."

" Again," said Mr. Walker, growing more than ever enthusiastic in his statements of figures and facts, which cannot be disputed, " just think, the wheat cultivation in the West, for 1909, was one million, one hundred thousand acres greater than in 1908, thus making a comparative increase in labor. This year, as I have said before, was saved by the grace of God in sending us such glorious weather for harvesting. Our harvests are short and sharp, and this year we will have an amazing return, easily reaching one hundred millions, and this is not all. Remember that this year's increase will be judged as a forecast for the increase of next year, and this labor problem has to be solved ahead of time."

Referring to the subject of the influx of American farmers which we had seen and heard so much of lately, particularly during our tour through the Okanagan Valley, and further west, Mr. Walker said : " We will receive seventy-five thousand people from the United States, this year, and according to the Custom's report the average wealth brought in by each, in cash, and agricultural implements, amounts to $1,000, so that the West has gained this year the astounding sum of seven millions, five hundred thousand dollars alone from these newcomers. These settlers are of the very best blood in the country from which they come, and are invariably experienced tillers of the soil. They are moving North because they have large families of grown-up sons, and they want to find homes for them in a territory where land sells from ten to twenty-five dollars per acre, in perference to that of their own states, which would cost them one hundred and fifty dollars. The increase of the American invasion in the West in 1909 was 64 p. c."

In estimating the wealth which the Americans are bringing into Canada, Mr. Walker states that he feels sure it is considerably above his figures, for most of the newcomers mention only a small proportion of what they really possess. As an instance of this assertion, he told of the presence in his office, a few days previous, of thirty men who had displayed $50,000 among them with which

211

they were looking over certain districts with the object of purchasing farms.

Another interesting point to which Mr. Walker drew our attention, was the sale of imported implements which, in binders alone in 1903, amounted to one million two hundred thousand dollars, and notwithstanding the rapid increase of the growth of the country with a proportionate increase of purchasers of such implements in 1908, they only amounted to eighty-five thousand dollars, but now that the Canadian manufacturers could not supply the demands for this year, the importations had increased since 1908 to $129,000.

While these figures were astounding to ponder over, they may be applied to all other requirements of the West, in this line, as may be judged by the importation of rakes, which in 1909 reached the sum of $247,-521, which in 1908 was only $18,312. These statistics only give us an idea of the enormous business that has developed in Canada in the manufacture of agricultural implements.

Mr. Walker also said that the manager of the Brantford Bolt & Screw Company had mentioned the fact to him that if his company had shipped to the West all the orders they received for these two small commodities during the spring of 1909, in one consignment, they would have filled a freight train of the Canadian Pacific

Railway, and as we have mentioned before this means anywhere from forty to fifty cars.

It is a country to dream about, to dream of what it will be in the future, with the great network of railways which will shortly cover it like a cobweb, of the hundreds of large and important cities, of the enormous trade between the provinces of the West alone, not to speak of the East, and what will be exchanged between the Atlantic and the Pacific, of the millions of population inhabiting this almost limitless area, of the development of the coal fields, the fruit farms, the wheat prairies, the lumber belts, and the opening of the scenic beauties of the different localities.

Such pictures never enter the mind of the Canadian in the East, but it does when he goes out West, and what is best about it all, is the fact that you do not want to run away from it, and you never misunderstand the Westerners. You believe all they say, for by the time you have spent twenty-four hours in the West, you are begining to think as they do, and when you have stayed a little longer, you find yourself suffering from a worse attack of optimism than all those you have met, and, probably it is a good thing you have to return to the East, in order to cool off a bit, or, there might be an explosion somewhere.

No better evidence of what we mean can

be given than in reproducing two prominently displayed signs we saw, one in Calgary and the other in Vancouver, The former read " There is no room for loafers in this hotel " and the other was in the office of a prominent railway man in Vancouver and read :

> " We stay up late, and early rise,
> Work like h—, and advertise."

1. Taking Visitors to view the Farms near Virden.
2. Sheep Ranch, Virden.
3. Experimental Farm, Brandon, Man.

CHAPTER XXIV

" New Canada and the New Canadians "

(Extract from " New Canada and the New Canadians " by Howard Angus Kennedy, published by Horace Marshall & Son, London, Eng., and Musson Book Co., Toronto.)

By the kind consent of the author and publishers of the above named book, I am enabled to make use of the following extracts. I would recommend the reading of this book to all who are interested in the Canadian West.   F. C.

" I entirely concur in the brief but express-ive description given to me by an English settler on the Assiniboine that the valley of the Red River, including a large portion belonging to its great affluent, is a " Para-dise of Fertility "... Indian corn, if pro-perly cultivated, and an early variety selected may always be relied on. The melon grows with the utmost luxuriance, without any artificial aid, and ripens perfectly before the end of August. Potatoes, cauliflowers and onions, I have not seen surpassed at any of our provincial fairs... The charac-ter of the soil in Assiniboia (now Manitoba) within the limits of the ancient (Lake Agas-siz) lake ridges cannot be surpassed. It is a rich black mould, ten to twenty inches deep, reposing on a lightish colored alluvial clay about four feet deep, which again rests on lacustrine or drift clay to the level of the water, in all the rivers and creeks inspected. As an agricultural country I have no hesitation in expressing the strongest conviction that it will one day rank amongst the most distinguished." (See page 22 S. J. Dawson.)

"In the city of Winnipeg alone there are now over 3,000 Icelanders, and you could scarcely pick them out from the rest of the population. Now and then they let the world know who they are. Their annual festival in August commemorates the granting of a constitution to Iceland by the Danish King in 1874 ; but the festival consists largely of the athletic sports familiar to us all. To be sure, there are speeches and choruses in Icelandic ; but these chant the praises of the new land, the 'foster-home,' as well as the old."

"The people are more than satisfied with their transplantation ; and with good reason. The winter is colder in Manitoba than in Iceland—which causes some surprise— but the summer is so much warmer and brighter as to put all comparison out of the question.

"There is a charming belief that the breaking up of millions of acres of hard prairie has caused a perceptible increase of the warmth radiating from the soil, so that autumn lingers, staving off the advent of frost. Prosaic folk hold that farmers have learnt to put in the seed earlier, and so avoid late ripening—that is all."

" Dogmatic assertions that you can go on taking heavy wheat crops off the land year after year without exhausting the soil are not convincing, extraordinarily rich though that soil is. Many of the farmers themselves are becoming healthily sceptical on this point, and either alternate their wheat with timothy and other grasses or allow the land to recuperate in summer fallow every year or two, with the best possible results. One of the most experienced, the owner of a thousand-acre farm, tells me that he has reaped 40 bushels per acre on land thus rested, while an adjoining field, where the grain had simply been sown on the ploughed-up stubble, only yielded half that quantity."

" It is a great mistake to imagine that all Manitoba is like the great flat treeless plain that the cursory visitor sees from a Canadian Pacific Railway car. If you strike north from Winnipeg, you soon escape from the bareness of the ' bald-headed prairie ; ' and as far as you like to go you will find the Province well wooded and well watered. There are even a number of gently sloping hills, which neighbourly affection honours with the name of mountains. Nature here is not sensational. For cliffs and cataracts you sigh in vain. Yet the current of the Winnipeg River already supplies electricity

to work the tramways of the Capital 60
miles away, and is capable of generating a
million horsepower whenever it is wanted."

"The charms of Manitoba are great, but,
without any depreciation of her buxom maturity, I turned my face to the West in search
of her younger sister. To the north-west,
I should say, at first, for on this occasion I
took the new route opened up by the Canadian Northern Railway Company. For the
first 250 miles the railway is still in the
'Premier Prairie Province,' with Lake Manitoba, Lake Dauphin and Lake Winnipegosis
far away on the right, and the slopes of Riding
Mountain on the left. The land is practically
all good, but a large part of it is covered
with scrubby poplar, and as long as there
is plenty of open prairie to be had the new
settler naturally lets the scrub land severely
alone,—unless, that is, he is a Galician."

"The next railway divisional point, called
Humboldt, is in the heart of a district largely
settled by German-Americans, who in their
second or third year have each from 80 to
100 acres under crop. South of Humboldt
there is a settlement of Mennonites, who
may be described as German-Quakers from
Russia, and some of these people at the
end of two years work have 100 to 150 acres
under crops."

"There is only one class on the plains,
and that is the working class. Here and

1. Branch from Plum Tree, Indian Head.
2. Flower Garden, Indian Head.

there you meet a gentleman of leisure, but he is called a tramp."

" A friend says : 'It makes one blush, as an Englishman,—the things done by fellows sent out often because they are unmanageable in England. The most useless men I ever saw were young fellows who were said to have had " the best education, " but were positive fools. They were so bull-headed they would not learn, they would not buckle down to work, but lived out among themselves on their ranches in filthy shacks and came into town to drink. They really got lower than any other class in the country. Yet there was a great deal of good in these black sheep ; and many of them, after flinging away their money, were dragged out of the mire by the stern grip of necessity and driven along the road of hard work to a goal of brilliant success."

" The American immigrants, as a whole, come in simply to make homes for themselves and their children. Some of them, however, while they come in as farmers, and do their duty by the land, do so with the deliberate intention of selling out as soon as they can do so at a high enough profit. One of these men took a free quarter-section, and brought a whole adjoining section from the Hudson's Bay Company for $2,624. or $4.10 per acre. Three years later, in 1905, he sold this purchased section, includ-

219

ing a $1,200 house, perhaps $400 worth of fences, and 200 acres under fall wheat, for $14,400, or $22.50 per acre. He then bought back the standing crop for a lump sum of $2.500 and threshed 7,000 bushels out of it, adding largely to his profit on the original sale. At last accounts he was ready to sell his 160 acres of homestead. Having ' made his pile ' in this easy way, he will either try to double it by similar operations further afield or return to a life of modest but comfortable retirement in the United States."

" It was only in 1894 that the first Galicians arrived, nine families in all. They sent home such good reports of the country that to-day there are about 75,000 of them thriving there."

" One of the most interesting and progressive of the special groups to whom Central Alberta is indebted for its new population is that of the Scandinavians in ' New Norway ', but that is sixty-five miles south .of Star, in the *hinterland* of Wetaskiwin on the Canadian Pacific line running south from Edmonton. You would hardly suppose from a pure Indian name like Wetaskiwin that you had arrived in a settlement of Norwegians."

" It seems really absurd to think of Edmonton as a city, the fur-trading outpost in the wilderness. But in 1901 the town had 2,626 inhabitants, and five years later that figure had risen to 11,167 ; while Strathcona, on the south side of the river, contained another 2,921. To this day furs to the value of a million dollars (£200,000) every year pour into Edmonton from a multitude of outposts in the north, to be sorted and packed for the markets of the civilized world : but there is nothing furry or wild in the city's appearance. The Hudson's Bay Company itself is represented to the outward eye, not by a log fort, but by a large department store, with the wares of Regent Street or Westbourne Grove displayed in plate-glass windows. There are about a dozen banks, some of them very creditable to their architects and doing such an amount of business that they have had to establish a clearing house. There are at least half-a-dozen churches—Methodist, Presbyterian, Anglican, Baptist, Lutheran, Roman Catholic—and probably more. There are good schools, one of which could hardly be criticized—unless by extreme economists—if reared in London and is at present used, after school hours, as a Parliament House by the Provincial Legislature. There is positively a municipal electric tramway at Edmonton—or will be before this book is many months old, as the contract for its construction has been signed *. The roads—well, the less said about

* Now in full operation.

the roads the better, when you write about a Canadian town, but Edmonton is now paving its streets with wood blocks from British Columbia. There are other points on which western townsmen generally preserve a discreet silence ; but the Edmontonians are so bent on avoiding the common ailments of municipal infancy that before long I expect to see perfect drainage and water supply figuring in large type in the municipal advertisements."

"The Far North ! If there is a spark of the adventurous in your nature it flames up when you turn your back on Edmonton, and look away to the north. What you see with your mortal eyes is merely a beautiful picture of river and meadow and woodland, but if you look beyond the visible you see an illimitable expanse of country where you might travel week after week, month after month, even year after year, always exploring and always discovering something new. There is a distant sound even about Athabaska Landing, but that is only the first little step of 100 miles on the northward trail. You would have to go another 400 miles as the crow flies before quitting the Province of Alberta and launching out on the unorganized wilderness of Mackenzie Territory. On the Peace River, about 400 miles north of Edmonton, you would find a fair sprinkling of settlers. Some, no doubt,

1. Apple Tree—Irrigated Garden, Shuswap.
2. Prize Exhibit, C. P. R. Irrigation Farm.

have taken land there as a speculation, and look year by year for the railway that is sure to follow sooner or later." ·

" At Fort Vermilion on the Peace River, 650 miles north of the United States, the Hudson's Bay Company has for years had a flour mill, grinding wheat grown on the spot."

" It is an undeniable fact that the arctic circle cuts right across Yukon Territory. It is equally undeniable, however, and a good deal more upsetting to current beliefs as to the climate of Northern Canada, that in this very Territory, on the 63rd parallel of lattitude, or about as far north as Iceland and Archangel, wheat of the finest quality ripens without difficulty."

" I have heard of an Englishman who complains that Canadians do a day and a half's work in a day."

" As a capital city, Regina, like Edmonton and Winnipeg, has political importance ; but the Westerner is too busy establishing himself on his new farm to trouble much about politics."

" The West is constantly surprising even those who know it best."

" At Strasburg, about 50 miles north of Regina on a Canadian Pacific branch line, is a settlement formed almost exclusively of Germans direct from the Fatherland. This, like the rest of the German settlements, is making excellent progress. On the same line, a little further east, in the Lipton district, is rather a curiosity in the shape of a Jewish agricultural colony. ' Very few of the Hebrew Immigrants of the past year ', says the chief immigration commissioner at Winnipeg, ' have settled on land permanently, but persist in remaining in towns or peddling goods about the country.' "

"The colony of Esterhazy, the first—born Hungarian settlement, is very prosperous, with large herds of cattle."

" A little log house and the humble inhabitants form as pleasant a picture as anything I witnessed in the whole journey. The man and his wife were both French-Canadians, and their presence on that far northern plain was a hopefully significant fact. One of the most painful features in the history of Canada for the last 30 year has been the exodus of French-Canadians from the Province of Quebec. It is believed that at least half a million of the two million French-Canadians are now to be found under the Stars and Stripes, though you might find it hard to identify a Jean Baptiste Lajeunesse and Dominique Lafortune under the new names of John Young and Washington Lucky. The greater number of these expatriated French-Canadians are to be found in the New England States, where they have supplied the labour for the cotton mills

224

and shoe factories of many a Massachusetts town. There was also, however, a large French-Canadian emigration, less permanent in intention, to the American North-West, and specially to Illinois and Michigan. Thousands of the inhabitants were, and still are, expert lumbermen, spending their winters, even when they have ·farms of their own in the St. Lawrence Valley, cutting and drawing timber from the northern forests. Such men as these found a great and profitable market for their labour in Michigan, a State which may indeed be said to have been transformed from forest to farmland by French-Canadian hands and axes. Hundreds, if not thousands of them are now being brought back into Canada, though not chiefly into their native Province, by the same economic force that is drawing northward hundreds of thousands of English-speaking Americans. These Americanized French speak English perfectly, though most of them French as well, and their names are generally spelt in the old French, though pronounced in English fashion."

" As for agriculture, few had any idea that crops would grow upon these (South Albertan) arid plains. The cattle-kings to whom great ranches had been leased by the Federal Government on easy terms were the undisputed and unenvied monarchs of the prairie. To-day the uninhabited prairies are dotted with homesteads, villages and towns. The arid immensities of brown bunch-grass and grey sage-bush are chequered with yellow fields of wheat. The cowboy is a curiosity. The cattle-king has abdicated and the farmer reigns in his stead."

" It is in Japan that a good many South Albertans expect to find the great future market for their wheat. The Japanese are taking to wheat instead of rice ; and the Americans have been supplying what they want in enormous quantities. Owing to the treatment of their fellow-countrymen in California, and to their cordial relations with the United Kingdom, the Japanese would naturally prefer to get their supplies from Canada. Unfortunately the only Canadian wheat-growers near enough to the Pacific sea-board to compete with the Americans have barely begun to develop their land, and their trans-Pacific trade is still but trifling in amount."

" The famous Cochrane ranch near Macleod, with its lordly domain of 66,000 acres, has been bought by a Mormon syndicate for subdivision into farms at a price ($6., or 25s., per acre) five times what Senator Cochrane paid for the land twenty years ago; and when I visited the place, I met two gentlemen, one English and the other Irish, who had just bought the remaining live-stock, about 10,000 heads, for a matter of $250,000 (£50,000).

CHAPTER XV

The Doukhobor Woman

(By Jean Blewett in " Collier's Weekly," and used by permission.)

" THE DOUKHOBOR woman is no Venus. A long while ago she acquired the habit of working, and, theorists to the contrary, hard, incessant work does not tend toward beauty of face or form.

"Taking her place at the plow when the first furrow is turned in the spring, planting, hoeing, making hay, harvesting the grain, threshing and grinding the same, doing the whole year round a man's work, has given her the figure of a man. She has muscles instead of curves; there is no roundness or softness visible. The sun has burned her face brown and her eyelashes white. Her hands and arms are the hands and arms of a working man. But her life in the open has done this for her, it has given her a dignity of carriage and a strength and wholesomeness more pleasing than mere beauty.

" *The Community Life*

" Her dress is peculiar—she is a peculiar person. She wears an exceedingly full skirt. Indeed, when you first see her you wonder why Peter Veregin, with his rigid ideas of economy, does not order a style of garment which will not call for a double quantity of material. With this goes a jacket tied in at the waist with an apron, which, like everything else about the Doukhobor woman, is of generous propertions. On her feet are heavy shoes, and on her head the unfailing white covering, which is nothing more or less than a square of cotton folded once and tied under the chin.

"The houses open on to a common court or dooryard, and in this the children are put to play and the bedding to air. Here in the evening the women gather with their embroidery frames to catch the last glimpse of sunlight for their work—pretty work it is and begininng to find a ready market. The hands holding the needle are coarse and hard from labor, but the flower and leaf which they bring out on the linen are dainty and exquisite as any lady of the land could do.

"What the hearth is to the family circle the court is to the community circle, a common meeting-place for those who will sit silent and those who will talk. You notice this, it is the old who do the gossiping, the young who do the laughing. The middle-aged Doukhobor, to quote the little Galician girl at the post, ' is of a sour face and still tongue.'

"At the upper end of the court is the store,

228

with its varied stock of merchandise ; at the lower end the bath-house, which is at once the village sanitarium and its pride. Here go the Doukhobors for a general cleaning up each Saturday evening. The fire on this altar of cleanliness never goes out. If a man falls ill, instead of having a doctor he has a bath. If a child is taken with croup, measles, whooping-cough, or any of these ailments, that child is rushed to the bath. Let a woman show the first symptoms of headache, backache, or nerves, and she is given a course, short but efficacious, in the ' health-house.'

" The place boasts a brick stove out of all proportion to its size, a stone bath, and a sweating-room. A great place for the curing of fevers contracted while working on the railway or in the woods, the rheumatism of the ditches, bronchial affections, any and all the diseases which show themselves.

" The houses, which run down each side of the street, are cleanly, comfortless places, as free from decoration as the women who preside over them. A place to eat in and sleep in, this is what the Doukhobor house is, and all it is. The fireplace, with its big oven, fills one end ; the table the other, and along the wall runs a wide bench.

" *The Luxury of Scrubbing*

" It is to be wondered at that these hard-working folk do not have some comforts in the home. A wise and sympathetic man who has done a great deal for them, and who has their confidence, said as much to them of late. They answered with a superior air that life was not made for comforts and ease-taking, but for work, much work. The bed is made upon the bench by the wall, and in the morning the housewife carries the mattress, quilts, and coverlets out of doors and spreads them on a structure built for the purpose. Thus is a double purpose served ; the bedding is aired in hygienic fashion, and the house is left free to the spinning of carded wool or the weaving of gorgeous rugs, or some of the other industries, which go on with unflagging zeal. After being with her, I know the Doukhobor woman's idea of heaven—a place where she will have a long stretch of golden street to scrub to her heart's content. It is her one luxury, scrubbing, and she never stints herself.

" She does not bother her head with cook-book or recipe. Her meals are like herself, substantial and wholesome. No flesh of fowl or beast, though prairie hens rear their broods on the outskirts of the village street, and, as for the wild ducks, no sooner is the song of the gun heard in the land than instinct prompts them to seek the ponds and creeks of the Doukhobor. Here, liter-

230

ally, none dare molest or make afraid—as more than one sportsman finds to his cost. The waters, black with teal, mallard, blue-bill, and red-head, offer a great temptation. He steals a shot, maybe two, but before he has time to gather up the spoil, the avenger is upon him. If he is descreet he stands not on the order of his going.

" Infuriated Amazons

"They are no respecter of persons. The story goes that a certain man, who was poobah of the place in the hollow of his hand, went forth one fair September morning to shoot in the Doukhobor grounds. Suddenly there came bearing down upon him a couple of stalwart women. The Doukhobor women did not care who or what he was. He had broken one of their laws, violated a tenet of their faith. They took his ducks away, they threw him and his gun in the pond. When he had choked and spluttered till purple in the face, they pulled him out, put him in his rig, gave him the lines, and started the horse off on a galop.

" 'Why didn't you put up a fight ? ' a friend asked him later. ' I wouldn't have taken that from any two women under the sun.'

" ' Women,' sighed the poobah, his pride all gone ; ' they weren't women—amazons, amazons, that's what they were.'

231

" The Doukhobor woman's house is home-made, so is her furniture. She puts her heavy plates on the bare board, and beside them wooden spoons carved by the lads of the village. She serves porridge made of wheat grown on their own land, ground in their own mill, and a big blue pitcher of milk from their own cows. There is a basin of potatoes, a platter of eggs, another of bread cut from the immense brown loaves which only the Doukhobor women know the secret of : and for a luxury there is tea—but only as a luxury.

" ' We eat not to pleasure in food, but to make strong,' says the Doukhobor woman.

" 'Meat is strengthening,' you tell her.

" 'Maybe, maybe,' she makes answer, with that slow, superior smile of hers ; ' but we keep from tire long time. People who eat the flesh of bulls and heifers they tire more soon than Doukhobor. Yes, yes, the boss man who build railroad track he tell you so, too. It is not meat that makes one keep the strong arm and young face ; it is the wind and sun and being among ground new plowed. Yes, yes, I think.'

" *The Austerity of Romance*

" The Doukhobor woman is eligible to membership in the council, which is a parliament of the people for the people. . . . This council

232

is the beginning and the ending of all that
pertains to law and order in the community.
It determines questions, judges cases, settles
disputes, adjusts wrongs. Its findings are
final.

"It was Peter Veregin who assigned to
woman a place in this important body.
'Our women work as hard for the community
as we do, are equally interested in its welfare
and prosperity. Why should they not have
a voice in the council ? '

"There is no romance in the life of a Doukhobor woman. From a sturdy child with drab-
colored braids and a solemn face, she grows
into a woman. The braids, still drab, are done
round her head, and she is no whit less solemn.
One day young Joseph, finding himself in
need of a helpmate—which means a willing
worker—takes her to his house. She is
his woman. He does not bind himself to
cherish and protect, she makes no contract
to love and obey. In fact, there is no cere-
mony in connection with the mating. They
know nothing about affinity, and, as for
marriages being made in heaven, the self-
sufficient Doukhobor would think it a reflec-
tion on his judgment and the woman an in-
fringement on her rights, so to speak.

"If you were to ask them if they loved
each other they would answer vaguely that
to love all people was good. That state
of mind or emotions which we call ' falling

in love,' with the acute joys and jealousies
which accompany it, is to them apparently
an unknown quantity. There may be a
faint partiality in some direction, but it is
a case of—

' Love me little, love me long,'

if it is love at all. They are willing to
become partners, but as for the, glow and
gladness, the melting glance and the wild
heart-beat, these form no part or parcel of
a Doukhobor mating.

" *Her Maternal Patriotism*

" Faithfulness, which means much in any
union, means more perhaps in this one con-
summated without the sanction of the law
of the land. There is this to be said, cases
of desertion are exceedingly rare.

" If he has not enough of sentiment, tem-
perament, call it what you will, to love his
own woman to distraction, he is not apt to
fall into the snare of loving some other
woman. And so with his helpmate. She
keeps the even tenor of her way, cooks his
meals, nurses the children which come to
the home, works late and early. Happy ?
Oh, well, happiness is a thing of comparison. If it were not Joseph it would be some
other, since to mate with a man and bear
children is a part of her duty to the community.

" Rome in her mightiest days did not mean more to the Roman matron than the community means to the faithful, if unlettered Doukhobor woman."

1. Herd of Cattle, Gull Lake, Sask.
2. Sheep Pen, Gull Lake, Sask.

CHAPTER XXVI

Growth of Western Canada

IN CONVERSATION with a representative of "Canada," Mr. Vere Brown, Chief Inspector of the Canadian Bank of Commerce, gave some interesting instances of the growth of Western Canada.

"Ten years ago," said Mr. Brown, "Winnipeg was the only point in the Prairie Provinces at which this bank had a branch, while to-day, of our 217 branches, ninety-six are in Manitoba, Saskatchewan, and Alberta. This might appear too great a measure of expansion, but the settlement of the country has rendered necessary an extraordinary increase in the number of branches of the Canadian banks. The fact is that the banks have difficulty in keeping pace with the development of the country. It is not a question of finding openings for branches, but of finding efficiently trained officers to man them.

"The building of railroads has proceeded at an enormous rate, as is evidenced by the issues of Canadian railway securities in the London market, but as far as the North-western Provinces are concerned the experience of the railroads has been similar to that of the banks—they have been under pressure to keep pace with the requirements of the country. In many parts of the West the building of branch lines of railway has been behind rather than ahead of the settlement of the land.

" As to the openings for employment in Canada, Mr. Brown said there is no doubt that good artisans can command employment there. There are plenty of opportunities, too, for young clerks of good capabilities, though the office man of thirty years and upwards would probably experience difficulty in finding an opening unless he possessed qualifications much above the average. There is a great demand everywhere for domestic servants, and the wages for this class of help are high. For the energetic young farmer, however, Western Canada —and, indeed, many parts of Eastern Canada —offers great promise. The man fitted to go on the land could scarcely fail to do well."

In reply to a question regarding the movement in real estate values, Mr. Brown said : " I have no hesitation in saying that, taking the country as a whole, the situation as to real estate values is quite a healty one— rather remarkably so, having regard to the rapidity of the country's development and the great prosperity it has been enjoying. There is no extended speculation in urban real estate. For example, in Toronto, which now has a population of 350,000, the price of property in the best residential districts is from $75 to $100 a foot frontage. $150 a foot frontage is about the highest price known for a choice property, whereas in the other near-by American city of Buffalo, with a population only about 25 per cent. greater, as much as $300 a foot has been paid for property on the best residential street. In Winnipeg a financial institution ten or twelve years ago paid about $40,000 for 52 feet on the Main street. Three years ago it paid $70,000 for 26 feet adjoining on the north, while a few months ago it had to pay $100,000 for 26 feet adjoining on the south—i. e., nearly $4,000 a foot. This fairly indicates the prevailing prices of the best central property there. They are regarded by many as too high, but when compared with values in Western American cities, such as Minneapolis, St. Paul, Seattle, Portland, etc., they are not remarkable, considering the great future which Winnipeg undoubtedly has. In one or two of the most advertised Western cities there has probably been some inflation, but it is mainly in connection with suburban building lots, and in any case the bearing of the matter is purely local.

"The banks in Canada do not lend on real estate, and the land mortgage companies only lend on central property to the extent of 50 per cent. of the valuation, so that

239

there is not much ammunition for any extended campaign of real estate speculation. I believe it is the opinion of bankers generally that the value of business property in most of the Western cities is too high, but whether they are or not depends upon how rapidly the settlement of the Western Provinces is effected, and it is a question whether this is not going to greatly exceed the anticipations of all but the most optimistic. The immigration to Canada last year was in the neighbourhood of 250,000, including a large propertion of well-to-do Western American farmers. This year it is expected to exceed 300,000, and, with the cheap agricultural lands in the United States pretty well all taken, it is not difficult to imagine the movement of European emigration being concentrated on Canada until these figures are increased to 500,000 or 600,000, or more, in a very few years. What this would mean to a country which now has a population of only seven or eight millions in all, it is difficult for anyone to properly appreciate.

" The Canadian investment field is at present in high favour with British capital, and it is, of course, of the utmost importance to us that this should continue to be so. There is, however, the danger that the existing conditions may render possible some undesirable flotations. The financial interests in Canada are deeply concerned to see the

British investor discriminate wisely in making his Canadian investments, and "Canada" ought to lose no opportunity of pointing out that through the London office of the Canadian banks it is at all times possible to obtain trustworthy information regarding Canadian securities. As far as this bank is concerned, we are always pleased to answer any enquiries from contemplating investors. Persons living out of London could have their own bankers write our London office for the required information.

"Mr. Brown also spoke of the great work which was being done for Canada by the Canadian Pacific Railway in the development of irrigated lands for a distance over 300 miles in the district between Calgary and Medicine Hat, covering an area of over 300,000 acres. This portion of the Province of Alberta is likely to become densely populated with specially selected settlers holding 80 or 100 acres each."

From " Canada " Jan. 15th 1910.

"The particulars of the project formed by the Canadian Pacific Railway Company of establishing settlers on ' ready-made ' farms on the irrigated lands of the company in Southern Alberta were fully set forth in a paper entitled ' Irrigation in Its Relation to Agriculture and Colonization,' read at the Royal Colonial Institute by Mr. C. W.

241

Peterson, General Manager of the Canadian Pacific Irrigation Colonization Company.

"Mr. Peterson, at the outset, insisted on the importance of irrigation, both from an economic and an imperial standpoint, giving it as his opinion that the ' general extension of irrigation in all the more important colonies of the Empire, with one or two possible exceptions, would be the means of creating an additional volume of national wealth, and, what is more important, prosperous homes, beyond the wildest dreams of the most sanguine Imperialist.' He noted with satisfaction the growing interest that was being taken throughout the Colonies in this subject, and passed on to a rapid sketch of the practice of irrigation in the history of the world, adding the significant comment that ' even' to-day seven-eighths of the entire food supply of the world is produced on irrigated lands.'

"The speaker declared that, while this process should be regarded as agricultural art of very wide application, its prominent association with the task of desert reclamation had blinded the public eye to its value for regions where such reclamation was not an issue. It was not, he pointed out, merely a recourse to ensure the safety of the crop, but had been found in practice to profitably push both growth and production, even where the natural moisture seemed ample.

" It is now an accepted theory," he added, " amongst soil chemists that the richest lands of the continent of America lie in the vicinity of the 100th meridian, where the rainfall is lowest.

" *The origin of the project.*

" It was then explained that, having in view the possibilities of the small farm under irrigation, and with a realization of the expediency of a stronger effort towards directing British immigration to Canada than that exerted in connection with the movement of people from other countries, the broad lines of an agricultural holdings plan were formulated, which it was expected would produce the desired result. 'The determining factor in respect to this new policy,' said the speaker, ' was the significant information brought to light in connection with the administration of the Small Holdings Act of 1907. It was learned that, although this legislation had only been in force for two years the enormous number of applications received thereunder, some 23,000, indicated an unmistakable tendency on the part of the people of Great Britain to ' return to the land.' When it is further considered that out of this enormous volume of applications it has only been possible to satisfy 1,500 ; furthermore, that only one-third of the number, or 500, have actually

obtained possession of their land up to date,
it was realized that there is a crying need
to be supplied, and that a large number of
people, now struggling for a bare existence,
could be returned to the land, and in a few
years become proprietors, and carve out for
themselves and their children a future that
would necessarily be vastly brighter than
anything they could legitimately hope for
at home.

" *The project in detail.*

"The basic principle of the project is to
' help the people to help themselves,' and
the class of colonists whom the company
will endeavour to interest is one that gives
reasonable promise of being successful and
independent, with which end in view the
conditions and restrictions surrounding the
scheme are to be designated. The company also believes in the small farm, and
for that reason the holdings will be limited
to from 80 to 100 acres of irrigable land.
or 160 acres of non-irrigated lands, situated
in the more humid belt of the West. An
important point mentioned is that, to make
the colonist almost immediately revenue
producing, it will be the aim of the company
to break up a portion of each holding, probably
from 40 to 60 acres, the year prior to his going
into occupation, so that there may be a
crop available a few months after he has

taken possession. This crop ought to provide a cash income during the first season,
varying from £100 to £250, according to
the season and the state of the grain market.

" It is the company's intention to settle
such colonist in units, up to sixteen families,
as it does not believe in unwieldy settlements,
an arrangement which will allow of adequate
social and educational facilities.

"Mr. Peterson further pointed out that
the interest of the company in these transactions does not cease with the final purchase
of a parcel of land, for the colonist will,
under the provisions of the project, become,
in a sense, ' a ward of the company,' whose
object it will be to ensure the success of each
individual settler by every means in its power.
With this idea a staff of lecturers and experts
will be at the disposal of those unfamiliar
with the handling of water, and at central
points farms will be operated to demonstrate
the possibilities of the irrigated tract ; in
short, everything will be done ' consistent
with the development of individual enterprise, without which no scheme of assisted
settlement can hope to meet with complete
success '. The project is practically an invi-
tation to approved colonists with agricultural experience to go into partnership with
the company, and a ' decided preference
will be given to married men with families ',

care being also taken to eliminate, as far as possible, the incident of failure.

"The prices at which the company's lands are at present disposed of vary from £3 to £8 per acre. It would perhaps be safe to estimate the land value of the average holding at from £600 to £750. It is estimated that the cost of erecting the necessary buildings, placing other improvements on the land, breaking, seed, etc., will amount to about £500. To this extent the company proposes to bear the entire financial burden on a ten-year repayment plan.

"The settler's own capital might advantageously be expended as follows:—For the purchase of the necessary live stock, £100 ; for furniture, household expenses, and horse feed, about £25 ; one-half the total cost of implements (the balance being repayable to the dealer at a future date), another £50 ; transportation to Canada, about £25 ; or a total of £200. The colonist with £200, or over, would, according to the above estimate, be starting under the most favourable auspices. If a settler had grown-up children who could assist in the farm work, and were willing to work out for wages part of the time during the first year or two, a somewhat smaller capital would suffice."

CHAPTER XXVII

Victoria and Vancouver Island

Wm. Blaynay in " Canada."

"TWENTY of the principal towns on the Island have banded themselves into a society called the Vancouver Island Development League, to co-operate in the work of publishing abroad the advantages and opportunities which the island offers to the settler. These advantages and opportunities are best enumerated in the words of the League: 'Fruit and vegetable growing, poultry raising, mixed farming, flower culture, bee-keeping, timber, pulp wood, coal, iron, marble, gold, copper, building stone, fire and brick clay, cement, quicksilver, salmon, herring, cod and halibut fisheries, sealing industry, deep-sea harbours, Government land, cheap electric power, water power, manufactures, railroad building, ship-building, the most equable climate in the world, unequalled living conditions, hunting and fishing, splendid roads, fine schools, law and order, the grandest and most varied scenery, the geographical command of trans-Pacific commerce, and the assembled essentials of manufacturing greatness.' Surely there are very few islands of 15,000 square miles (about twice the size of Wales), either within the British Empire or without it, that can boast of so many natural resources and attractive features. Anything cultivated in Great Britain will grow and flourish equally as well in Vancouver Island, and all domestic animals thrive and can be profitably ' raised ' there.

" Vegetables, in some cases, grow to enormous proportions in the virgin soil. Mr. Ernest McGaffey, Secretary of the Victoria Branch of the Development League, had occasion to visit the small town of Duncan's, some forty miles from the capital, and was invited to dine with one of the most prominent farmers there. ' Do you like carrots, Mr. McGaffey ? ' asked his host. ' Why, sure," was the reply. ' Here, boy,' called the farmer to one of his employees, ' go and fetch a carrot from the field.' A few minutes later the boy returned, carrying on his back a carrot of gigantic size. This he placed on the ground, and with an axe cut off a small portion, sufficient for the wants of the household and its guest for the meal, and carried it to the kitchen.

" Big vegetables of this description are not, however, the exception in British Columbia they are the rule. Mr. McConnell, editor of the Vancouver *Saturday Sunset*, told me that he had recently purchased a quantity of potatoes grown in the Similkameen Valley, the majority of which were so large that it was necessary to cook only one for each

248

dinner for his household of four or five people. I myself saw pumpkins weighing half a cwt., swedes of larger size than I have ever seen in Great Britain, and potatoes weighing 2, 3, and 4 lbs. each, all grown in the Chiliwack Valley. The two valleys I have mentioned are, of course, on the mainland, but this makes no difference. The same vegetables will grow to the same proportions and with the same excellent flavour equally as well on Vancouver Island.

" Whilst on the subject of vegetables, it is interesting to note that the Victoria Fruit Growers' Exchange, which by no means includes all the growers on the island, last season handled 1,000 boxes of tomatoes, 200 boxes of peas, and 1,000 sacks of potatoes, besides large quantities of asparagus, carrots, squash, corn (Indian), turnips, citrons, cucumbers, beans, radishes, lettuce, onions, etc.

" Turning from vegetables to fruit, the Exchanges handled 480,000 boxes of strawberries, 24,000 boxes of currants, 2,000 crates of cherries, 4,300 crates of prunes, 24,000 boxes of loganberries, 14,400 boxes of gooseberries, 3,000 crates of plums, 20,000 boxes of apples, 1,000 crates of rhubarb, and 1,000 boxes of pears. From this it will be seen that strawberry culture forms one of the most important branches of fruit growing ; it is destined to increase to a distinctly large and profitable industry, by reason of size and delicious flavor of the berries.

"Much attention is also being paid to the cultivation of bulbs and flowers as profitable industries, and bee-keeping has met with considerable success. The Island is particularly suitable for poultry-raising, and farmers have no difficulty in making each bird return an average profit of $2 a year."

"*Okanagan Valley.*

"The fruit lands in many instances lie on the sides of hills sloping down to valley or river at all kind of angles. Some of these slopes are so steep that one can almost credit the story, current in the West, of a party of tourists who while making a boating trip on one of the lakes, were suddenly startled by a great splash in the water ahead of them. On rowing up to the spot, a man's head appeared above the surface, and a voice exclaimed, 'This is the third time I've tumbled out of that durned orchard to-day!'

"The views to be obtained in the valleys of British Columbia are exceedingly striking. One may stand among a patch of fruit trees—awaiting but the rise of the sap to put forth blossom and leaf—and look over the ground sloping from one's feet down to a magnificent stretch of water, glittering in the bright winter sunlight, or reflecting the foreshore of the opposite bank. Here again run rows upon rows of fruit trees, behind which rise the eternal hills, their growth of fir and other coniferous trees adding to the majesty of their outlines. I found some of the most interesting views in the ' bench ` land ' of the Okanagan Valley. Here one may trace with the eye the banks of prehistoric highwater marks, falling away like steps to the present level of the lake which has given the valley its name. The water, as it receded from each " bench,' left behind a deposit of rich alluvial earth, which has won for British Columbia in general, and the Okanagan Valley in particular the fame of being one of the best fruit-growing countries in the world.

" Earl Grey, whose ability to sum up a situation happily and correctly is well known and appreciated here, paid a great tribute to the industry of fruit-growing in this Province during his tour two years ago. This has often been quoted, but it so truly fits the case that I venture to give it again. Said his Excellency:— ' Fruit-growing in your Province has acquired the distinction of being a beautiful art as well as a most profitable industry. After a maximum wait of five years, I understand the settler may look forward with reasonable certainty to a net income of from $100. to $150. per acre, after all expenses of cultivation have been paid.'

251

" Here is a state of things which appears to offer the opportunity of living under such ideal conditions as struggling humanity has only succeeded in reaching in one or two of the most favoured spots upon the earth. There are thousands of families living in England to-day, families of refinement, culture, and distinction, who would be only too glad to come out and occupy a log hut on five acres of a pear or apples orchard in full bearing, if they could do so at a reasonable cost.

" The fruits which do well are principally apples, pears, plums, prunes, cherries, strawberries, raspberries, blackberries, and gooseberries, while such tender varieties as grapes and peaches are grown successfully in the more sheltered and southernmost district.

" Now as to the question of cost of lands and length of time before the new grower is assured an income. ' Unimproved ' fruit lands—by which is meant the land in its natural state, uncleared of timber, and, in some instances, stones and rock— is purchasable, usually on easy terms, at from $75 (£15) to $125 (£25) per acre. Improved and irrigated lands are, of course, more in proportion. When the trees of an orchard have reached maturity, the profits attached to a crop of fruit are said to range between $500 (£100) and $1,000 (£200) per acre ; but these prices, of course, must necessarily depend upon a variety of happy circumstances."

"The following statement as to the cost of setting out twenty acres of apple trees was furnished to me from an official source :—

"Twenty acres (irrigated) at $150 per acre......	$3,000	00
Fencing........	200	00
Preparing land.........	250	00
Trees (968), at 25 cents each............. ..	242	00
Freight, etc...........	22	00
Setting out trees, at 8 cents each..........	77	44
	$3,689	44

"The cost of cultivation, including pruning, spraying, irrigation, etc., after the first year, will amount to about $37 per acre per annum. Root crops and small fruits, planted between the trees for the first year or two, and red clover up to the fifth year, should more than pay for the trees ; but many fruit-growers deprecate this practice, preferring to devote the whole strength of the soil to the young trees. The fourth year the trees should produce some fruit— probably $100 worth. The cost of maintenance for five years, with the original cost and interest, would amount to $7,296.14, or $364.80 per acre, less the value of fruit produced. In the sixth year the orchard should produce $850 worth of fruit, in the seventh $3,200, and in the ninth $5,800, after which it should pay a net annual profit of $125 to $150 per acre—an assured income of $2,500 to $3,000 a year.

" In the case of smaller fruit, strawberries, I am told, realise a clear profit of from $400 to $500 per acre, when they can be gathered and packed for the market ; but I was also told of instances where they were grown at a loss, although the crop was plentiful, because no one could be hired to help to pick them."

Nelson, B. C.

" Some people like to call Nelson the ' Granite City ' ; others, who think it the best-lighted city in British Columbia, term it the ' Electric City.' Nelson, with its population of 7,000, owes its prosperity, its advancement, its well-being, its very existence, to three industries— mining, lumbering, and fruit-growing; though apparently, only one of these — mining — finds a place in the official seal of the Corporation of the City of Nelson. It is named in honour of a former Lieutenant-Governor of British Columbia, and is built on the side of a Mountain overlooking the west arm of Kootenay Lake.

1. Rossland, B.C.
2. Street in Rossland.
3. Nelson, B.C.

"Nothing can surpass the scenic beauty of its situation. Mountains tower above the city on all sides, while at its foot lies the calm blue water of a beautiful lake. So completely is the city imprisoned by the mountains that it is next to impossible for a would-be criminal to get away undetected from the immediate neighborhood. The Board of Trade, in whose office, which is nothing more than a wooden bungalow, I noticed a long shelf loaded with silver cups, silver trophies, and other prizes, to the value of many hundreds of dollars, with nothing between them and a would-be thief but the glass in the windows and a door whose lock could be easily opened with the aid of a bit of wire, A chance remark on the evident security of unprotected property in Nelson, and my surprise at seeing so much valuable silver ware in such an unsafe, unguarded position, led to the reply that ' they were all perfectly safe, and even if they were stolen, the thief could never get away from Nelson without being caught. Subsequent investigation of the city's position proved the correctness of the statement. There are only three ways out of the place : by the railway, by the lake, or over the mountains. The first two are easily watched, the third is impossible.'

" *Local industries.*

" When in Nelson, it is possible to live in a house of local granite and marble, or in one constructed of locally grown lumber turned out of the local saw-mills ready for the carpenter ; it is possible to sleep on a mattress placed on a spring frame both of which were made at a local factory ; it is possible to eat jam made at a local factory from locally grown fruit, and to smoke locally made cigars manufactured from British Columbian tobacco ; it is possible to drink beer brewed at the local brewery from British Columbian hops and Albertan barley ; it it possible to warm your house with stoves, furnaces, or grates made at the local iron-foundries ; it is possible to go out on the lake in a steamer, launch, motor-boat, row-boat, yacht, house-boat, or canoe, each one of which has been built on the spot.'

" The hotel accommodation at Nelson is excellent, and far superior to that of many Canadian towns of larger size. The Canadian Pacific Railway station is also a model of excellence in every way. In addition to the Canadian Pacific Railway, the city has the benefit of a branch line of the Great Northern running in from the States."

" *Nelson's climate.*

" Nelson is able—truthfully, I believe— to boast of its climate. It has no extremes :

excessive summer heat is tempered by cool breezes from the lakes, and during the winter its mountains protect it from cold, frost-laden winds. A street railway will be in operation in the city before many months have passed, although its usefulness will of necessity be confined to certain thoroughfares more or less adapted to this form of transportation. Abundant power for all purposes is supplied by the municipality from its hydro-electrical plant at Bonnington Falls, on the Kootenay River, nine miles away, where provision is made for greater development as it is required.

"The visitor to Nelson is almost unable to realise, until the matter has been explained to him, the difficulty which has been encountered and successfully surmounted in building up such a charming city on the side of a mountain. In Nelson the task has been no mean one. Creeks 30 feet deep have been filled in, mountain torrents curbed or diverted, retaining walls 30 feet in height built, hills and rocks planed down and whole streets excavated out of solid rock 20 feet in depth. There is now very little indication in the neat, orderly, well-kept appearance of the city and its streets and walks of these almost herculean undertakings. Building operations are continually proceeding, and the city is being built up in handsome substantial style, granite and marble being used in the construction of all the larger buildings. In addition to its local resources, the city is the business and judicial centre of the Kootenay district, and branches of several of the more important banks have been established in the city.

"A further recommendation of Nelson as a place of residence is the fact that excellent fishing is obtainable in the district, while the sportsman who finds his chief enjoyment behind dog and gun can bring home large bags of small game from the slopes of the hills surrounding the city."

ImTheStory.com

Lightning Source UK Ltd.
Milton Keynes UK
UKOW06f1859180617

303624UK00014B/208/P